INTER-CASTE AND INTER-COMMUNITY RELATIONSHIP

Developing Patterns

Inter-Caste and Inter-Community Relationship

DEVELOPING PATTERNS

M.K.A. SIDDIQUI

Commonwealth

Inter-Caste and Inter-Community Relationship : Developing Patterns

Edition : 2026

ISBN 81-7169-260-5

***Published by* :**
COMMONWEALTH PUBLISHERS (P) LTD.
4831/24, Govind Lane,
Ansari Road, Darya Ganj,
New Delhi - 110002
Ph. : 23272541, 23242541
e-mail : commonwealthpublishers2016@gmail.com

Distributed by :
ARJUN PUBLISHING HOUSE
4831/24, Govind Lane,
Ansari Road, Darya Ganj,
New Delhi - 110002
Ph. : 23272541, 23242541
e-mail : arjunbooks2001@gmail.com

Laser Typesetting by :
Dimple Computers
Delhi

Printed at :
Balaji Digital Press
Delhi

Acknowledgement

I am deeply indebted to Prof. Surajit Chandra Sinha, Ex-Vice Chancellor, Viswa Bharati University and former Director, Centre for Studies in Social Sciences for encouraging me to undertake the present study. Without the inspiration that I received from him this work would have not been possible.

I also owe a particular sense of gratitude to Dr. Kumar Suresh Singh, Director-General, Anthropological Survey of India for allowing me necessary facilities in the office of the Anthropological Survey of India. Centre for Studies in Social Sciences allowed me affiliation to their office which greatly facilitated my work. I express my thanks to the Centre for the same.

I would be failing in my duty if I do not record my gratitude to Indian Council of Social Science Research, New Delhi for providing me Senior Fellowship and necessary financial support for the work.

I had started the field work for the present study in the beginning of 1988 and was supposed to complete the write up by the middle of 1990, but had considerable set-back on account of communal disturbances in Bhagalpur, the field of my study, from October 1989 to January 1990, in which my camp was affected and some amount of valuable data was lost. I regret that this retarded the progress of my work considerably. I am thankful to the Director, ICSSR for allowing me time to reassemble the data and prepare a meaningful report, though this may perhaps be qualitatively not as good as the one I had planned before the communal disturbances.

I also acknowledge with thanks the valuable information given to me by Late Jogeswar Mandal, Chairman, Bhagalpur Co-operative Society, Shri Binod Kumar Verma, Gram Panchayat Supervisor; Jagdishpur: Shri Joginder Pandey and Shri N.N. Pandey of Phulwaria and a large number of people in the villages and the city of Bhagalpur. Shri Jawed Ejazul Haque has done the typing of the manuscript which I thankfully acknowledge.

M. K. A. SIDDIQUI

Contents

List of Tables

1

Introduction

Inter-relationship between various groups in a multi-ethnic situation is not permanently a static phenomenon. It is rather dynamic and often changing, under the impact of changed situations. It, however, assumes a pattern over a given point of time and under a given set of conditions, only to change when a new set of conditions are introduced into the total system or the structure of the society.

In a multi-cultural and multi-ethnic situation as that of our country, communities like Hindus, Muslims, Sikhs, Christians, Buddhists, Jains, to mention only a few, with their varied segments, live side by side and are bound to have some kind of relationship with each other. These relationships are likely to undergo changes over a number of years in response to changes in social, economic and political spheres. Inter-relationship between various castes within the stratified Hindu society as also between the various segments of some other communities, have been undergoing subtle changes.

A change within the internal structure of an ethnic group or a community, particularly as decisively large as that of the Hindus is not unlikely to have an impact on other communities or ethnic groups, constituting a part of the total environment.

Inter-relationship in a multi-ethnic situation assumes a pattern when a significantly large number of people belonging to one group has a particular kind of relationship with the other, though a few individuals belonging to respective groups may be involved in a kind of relationship that may not fit in the general pattern.

The scope of inter-relationship is fairly wide one. It may cover several aspects of life including economic, social, political, cultural etc. Economic relationship includes agrerian relations, employer-employee relationship as also relationship of rendering and receiving specialised services. Social relationship is usually governed by caste and class and, equality or inequality of statuses of the respective individuals and groups within the caste and class structure. Membership of a village community also occasionally binds people into a kind of relationship. Political relationship may involve not only the membership of political parties or their support but also ones involvement in factions as well as village councils and panchayat. Identification or difference in matters of belief and practices or patron-client relationship in the performance of rituals is yet another dimension of relationship in the domain of religion and culture. The aspect of relationship reflecting co-operation, friendliness, indifference or antagonism in the behavioural as well as in the attitudinal scale is also an important aspect of relationship between groups in the context of the region and neighbourhood.

Certain aspects of relationship are by nature more stable than others. These are resistant to change and when a change is introduced through external agencies, it may result in tension and conflict. Economic inter-relationships between various classes, particularly in a traditional society, are by nature persistent and stable and any attempt to alter the class structure amounts to a revolutionary change involving serious conflicts in the society. Caste based relationships are permanently fixed features and are relatively unchangeable, except perhaps, in a limited way, through long drawn mobility movements and 'sanskritization'. Some other kinds of relationship are of relatively ephimeral nature and comparatively easier to alter. These may relate to the domain of opinions and attitudes involving bias, prejudice and superstition.

The present study has a limited scope in the sense that it will involve a preliminary observation of the changing pattern of relationship between various categories of castes, grouped for the sake of convenience, into 'forwards', 'backwards' and 'Harijans'. An attempt will also be made to observe the impact of inter-caste relationship on inter-community, more specifically, Hindu-Muslim relationship. Our observation will be focused mainly on changes introduced or sought to be introduced into the socio-political and agrarian systems mainly through constitutional, legislative and administrative measures. The segments of society favouring and opposing these changes and their movements whatsoever may be worth noting.

Contacts in cities tend to be largely secondary and impersonal and as such the traditional norms of the society get obscured in the din and bustle of city life. In rural areas, on the other hand, contacts are predominantly primary and relationships are comparatively more stable and durable. Social change which may be observed to be occurring in the rural setting, may reflect the reality with a larger measure of certainty and authenticity, though city life may not be absolutely free from the manifestations of the aspects of traditional norms.

Not only the conspicuous presence of the caste factor in its traditional form but also the opportunity of observing social life in a more natural setting motivated our selection of the rural area as the field of our study, though the impact of developments in urban centres on rural areas may not be ruled out altogether.

The Background

The rural population in Bihar, as in most other parts of the country, is generally characterised by the presence of a number of well defined and elaborately structured groups. They are either castes, within the Verna jati system of the Hindu Society or pretty long established caste-like ethnic groups, more specifically those belonging to Muslim Community. These Hindu Castes and Muslim ethnic groups live side by side in multi-ethnic villages and sometimes in their exclusive settlements, not far off from each other. Hindu and Muslim Castes and Castes-like groups have been associated in villages for centuries, constituting almost a moral order.

The history of the association of Hindus and Muslims in a common habitat is so long that very few among its inhabitants can trade its origin. It exists in the memories of the people living in these settlements as a permanent feature and it is on account of this long association that a pattern of relationship has been built up and has been persisting through centuries. This traditional pattern of relationship is characterised not only by mutual acceptance but also by functional interdependenc in the context of the village and the region.

While the system of caste, a unique institution in vogue from time immemorial, has unmistakably provided a religio-philosophical basis for a pattern of interaction between various jatis in a village or region, the pattern of interaction between the jatis and the ethnic groups, outside the pail of the Verna-jati system, namely the Muslims has been largely based on their functional and class categories which reflect their respective backgrounds.

The 'secular' functionaries of the Hindu jatis and Muslim ethnic groups, organised on caste and caste-like patterns respectively, have traditionally been freely rendering and receiving specialised services and the resultant pattern of functional inter-relationship has inter-locked them into a larger system that has enjoyed remarkable stability, almost presenting the picture as a moral community. Yet the distinction between the groups directly involved into the Verna-jati system of caste on the one hand and those outside the system on the other, has remained glaringly obvious.

The distinction between the two main categories is not very difficult to discern. In the case of the Hindu jatis, the hierarchical pattern of the caste has an ideological basis, fully imbeded in the belief system, receiving nourishment from their own story of human creation supporting a hierarchical stratification of the society. But it is not so in the case of the Muslim ethnic groups, cherishing a different story of the creation of mankind as a part of their belief system and the eglitarian nature of the concept of society in Islam, though the structural elements of the system of caste have been found to be present among them. This is either due to the persistence of their pre-Islamic past or due to the dominance of the environment. Thus in case of the Muslims the hierarchy does not have an ideological basis, and may even run counter to their cultural ethos and as such it is not operative in their religious institutions. The caste-like features of the Muslim society which are found to be operative in a limited sphere of their society may also be the result of a variety of factors including intra-community and inter-community functional relationships in a situation where occupations are traditional and are rated high and low, as also the determination of status is on the basis of ascriptive characteristics.

Caste among the Hindus and Muslims are distinguishable in another respect. Mobility movement in the former takes the course of sanskritization or progressively greater imbibation of the Brahminical norms for gaining higher status in the Hindu Society. In case of the Muslims it assumes the process of Islamization. Sanskritization involves initiation of the life ways of higher status groups, in the caste hierarchy in concrete sense, while Islamization involves progressive assumption of Islamic style of life in the abstract sense.

Thus despite demonstrating an analogus structural similarity with the system of caste, the Muslim ethnic groups continued to constitute a distinct community in the cultural sense and in several respects have been markedly distinguishable from the Hindu caste and jatis. The two communities have also their exclusive domains of interaction and have distinct boundaries of their own.

It may, however, be added that the distinction between the two communities has been somewhat more pronounced on the level of perception, than on account of the actual divergence of their respective social systems as operationally observable. This accentuation of the perception of self-identity can be illustrated and exemplified from the behaviour pattern of the two communities in the past as well as at present. From a distinct trend of synthesis, at least at some levels of the two communities in the past, there is a growing emphasis on their distinctiveness at present.

Focussing on the Hindu Society, we observe that the pattern of inter-action between the jatis has traditionally reflected the religio-philosophical basis of the Verna-jati complex. It has shown a strong persistence of the deeply held belief in the binary opposition of 'pure' and 'impure'. This is reflected in a large measure in the structure of the society. This has also roughly coincided with the emergence and persistence of economic classes of 'upper' and 'lower' strata in the society. The passive acceptance of 'purity' and 'impurity' by all concerned has remained a long established tradition. Mobility movements, sanskritization, movement for a large scale combination to achieve political dominance, as well as frequent fissions have been some of the processes seeking to alter the persisting patterns at a given point of time and in specific areas, but on the whole the system itself has retained its basic structural framework, its pattern of inter-group relationship as also the philosophy that supports this hierarchical structural arrangement. During a long history of the people of India, preceding independence, the element of conflict, whatsoever, in the caste system, has been more latent than manifest.

The socio-cultural system of caste and its associated class structure, in a broad sense has remained stable by and large during a very long history of autocratic and colonial rule. The feudal and zamindari systems, in a general sense, the reinforcing and supporting pillars of autocracy and colonial rule, have provided congenial environment for the persistence of the system of Caste. The mediaeval and subsequently colonial rulers, despite their enormous power and authority, did not interfere with this ancient institution of caste to the extent of undoing the system or affecting a major change in the same.

While it cannot be denied that association with a community, namely Muslims, relatively free from caste taboos, had the effect of raising questions within the Hindu Society at least in some reflective minds, as to the appropriateness of the rigidity of the caste system a and had resulted in the emergence of certain sects like Vaishnavism, Kabirpanthi, Dadupanthi etc., yet it had no over all effect of change in the system. These sects at best represent some break-away groups and no more. Major protest movements like Jainism and Buddhism in more distant past have only a transient effect in the land of their origin and have been swept aside by counter revolutionary forces of Brahminism and caste based society. Such factors as the spread of modern education, development of communication, emergence and growth of large urban centres etc. have promoted a pattern of inter-action somewhat beyond the limiting condition of the caste system. The change has, however, been peripheral and the core has not accepted modifications to any notable extent.

With the dawn of independence the political philosophy of democratic egalitarianism received tremendous re-inforcement. The constitution of India fully reflects the anxiety of political leaders, generally with the background of modern education, to introduce a system that discourages institutionalised inequality. The strategies of social transformation as enshrined in the constitution, though not aggressively radical, seek to transform the society in India into a secular, democratic and egalitarian social order. Though the socio-political and administrative system prior to independence was not based on institutionalised inequality with all its ruthlessness, yet the society operated along this line. The strategies of social change as adopted by the constitution of independent India was a fundamental departure from many aspects of the traditional patterns which were included into the principles of hierarchy, antiquated customs and feudalism.

Thus 'theoretically' not only the idea of superiority and inferiority, involved in inter-group interactions, as embodied in the ethics of the caste system, stood challenged, but also the age old economic and political dominance of the privileged castes faced a formidable threat. Whether the founding fathers of the constitution of modern India really had the intention as well as the resources to change the structure of the society by introducing drastic reformatory measures to ameleorate the condition of the weak and the downtraden may be debatable, yet it was perceived with alarm by the privileged class, and vested interest began making preparations to preserve its position of dominance. Legislative measures for the removal of untouchability, abolition of the zamindari system, imposition of a ceiling on agricultural land and equitable distribution of resources and opportunities at the disposal of the state or job reservation for the Scheduled Castes and Backward Castes was deemed as a threat to dislodge the upper castes from the position they were enjoying for ages. These measures also implied the emancipation of the underdog who had until then been exploited by the land owners belonging to the privileged class. The land owning class, generally having the background of upper castes were alarmed and were up on the heels.

Anxiety of a section of political leadership to build an image of itselfas modern as well as its political interest, involved in obtaining mass support for the sake of gaining political power, were among factors that motivated many in the upper categories of caste and class hierarchy to lend support to such a radical idea, yet the real economic interest of the upper classes ran counter to the philosophy of egalitarianism. Lending support to radical ideas, largely for political reasons provided those in the higher achelons of society, with an opportunity to maintain their dominance over the political system. The newly acquired political power more than compensated the loss on other counts.

The political leadership was completely aware of the anxieties of the members of their own class and often had sympathies for them. They could not be expected to be radical enough to alter the structure of the society to the disadvantage of the class they belonged to. The situation was not unlikely to retard the process of change as stipulated in the constitution. She constitutional guarantees that were provided to the Scheduled as well as the Backward classes were initially for a period of twenty years in the hope that the gulf between the privileged and underprivileged will be bridged, but after a lapse of the two decades the achievement was insignificant enough to warrant the extension of the constitutional safeguards for another twenty years.

The manner in which the much propagated measures for the ameleoration of the condition of the Harijans and the Backwards are being implemented and the nature of the controversies and contradictions that have come to the surface do not provide justification for the hope of an early solution of the problem. It has further complicated the relationship and hardened attitudes.

At the upper level of the caste hierarchy, generally coinciding with the privileged class, the new state policy, devised under the constitutional provisions, was perceived as threat to the structure of the society. It was considered as a policy seeking to redistribute resources and to dislodge the privileged from the position of dominance it had occupied from a very long time.

At the lower level the new state policy raised level of expectation and brought about considerable consciousness about their rights. Since no significant change was visible or what little change that occurred was extremely insignificant, this was all perceived as false promise. They saw the upper classes as standing against improvement of their condition and opposed to their liberation from the position of subordination they were subjected to. The ritual inequality that was sought to be reduced through removing restrictions on temple entry was meaningless because the superimposed as well as self-imposed restrictions continued without any obvious threat to orderly life. The zamindari abolition effected through protracted and long drawn legal battle between the Zamindars and the Government did not materially benefit the deprived sections in any significant manner because the Government became the Zamindar and the bureaucracy comprised mainly of the upper castes. The land ceiling act was difficult to be implemented and in no case the surplus land went outside the caste and their kinsmen. Similar difficulties were encountered in proper application of the much propagated job-reservation for the underprivileged castes and its benefits, in whatever small measure were available, remained confined to a small section of the scheduled and backward communities. The net result was disappointmen , frustration and accentuation of tension among these deprived castes. They saw themselves in opposition to the forward castes.

As the state set before itself the 'secular' objective of trading along a long and hazardous path to 'equalise' all in a stratified caste society, with the kind of human and material equipments at its disposal, we notice that more problems emerged than could be solved. What little could be achieved during these four decades of independence was hightened expectations among the underprivileged and a feeling of frustration and resentment on account of the non-fulfilment of these expectations. The previleged felt seriously threatened in the wake of the formulation of the much propagated policy of reallocation of resources and opportunities. The situation introduced and accentuated an element of conflict, sometimes quite manifest, in the inter-relationship between the priviledged and underpriviledged, grouped on caste lines.

The two systems namely 'democratic egalitarianism' and the traditional caste system with its 'institutionalised inequality' and the values enshrined within the respective systems are diagonally opposed to each other and are mutually disjunctive. The two systems do not form a continuum. A change from one system to the other is very likely to generate conflict. It is difficult to conceive that both the systems will co-exist as part of the larger system in the society, retaining their originality or basic characteristics. Their confrontation is either likely to subvert the other or both have to undergo changes so that neither retains its original form. The nature and extent of change in either or both the systems will depend upon the relative strength of the two in different situations.

Thus the confrontation of 'democratic egalitarianism' and 'institutionalised inequality' in a society was bound to cause disequilibrium in the structure of the society. The former seeks to alter the existing socio-economic order and the latter endeavours to preserve the order, though often in somewhat modificd form. The sharpening of the latent competitive instinct between the privileged and the underprivileged castes, as a result of the changed situations, regrouped the castes into distinct competitive categories of the Forward or twice born, the Backward or the clean caste and the Harijan or the so called untouchables, significantly under thc various levels of development and also of purity and impurity. This does not mean to say that a number of castes within each category are respectively free from differences among themselves in many respects. However, their common categorisation became all the more a reality when the state grouped them in this manner to deal with their respective development and other related problems.

Considerable amount of literature has been generated on change in the caste system. A concept of 'compartmentalisation' was used to illustrate how caste responds to inevitable force of 'modernisation'. But this concept does not fully comprehend all the arenas of inter-caste interrelationship, particularly of the nature of domination and subordination. A change in this sphere is unlikely to occur without introduction of the element of conflict.

There are also references to 'caste' and 'democracy' and it is argued that social institutions in India have traditionally enjoyed autonomy. This is seen as a reason why India has survived as a democraey(Kothari – 10 : 1970). The question as to whether our social institutions were really democratic has not been satisfactorily answered. In fact if we look at the system of caste in the context of inter-caste relationship or inter-action between two groups it will provide evidence that all these groups militated against the very concept of democracy and democratic egalitarianism. They will appear to be designed to exclude and exploit the weak. Even at the village level the panchayat has traditionally been dominated by certain caste or castes in control of resources. The position of those not in control of resources has always been at a low level (Buch – 1988).

It will be wrong to suppose that caste is adverse to change has not accepted modification over a number of years. In fact change of far reaching consequences has occurred into the system. Besides modification in the rules governing physical contact and commensality or acceptance of food and water, which are peripheral, some very drastic changes have occurred. Caste has frequently shown the tendency of decline as a ritual. It also seems to have loosened its grasp in holding fast to feudalism but it has adequately compensated itself in asserting with full force in politics and in concentrating power in its own hands. Thus with every change it emerges stronger than before.

The introdcuction of tension and conflict on caste lines is obviously a matter of concern for the dominant in the caste society. This not only goes against the ethos of the caste system but also weakens its hold on the vast bulk of the underprivileged, subjected to exploitation by their overlords. There is a need for their mobilisation with a view to forging unity in the economic and political interest of their traditional patrons.

Politically motivated 'system maintaining cultural elites' of the caste society alarmed at the situation are expected to devise methods to restore their dominating influence throughstri ving to eliminate inter-jati conflict. Restoration of inter-jati harmony is obviously possible through persistent emphasis on the basic elements of common culture as distinct from other cultures. Those striving to maintain the hegemony of the traditionally dominant, through re-establishing inter-jati harmony, may have to lay stress on emotionality, suppressing, ignoring or side-tracking the problems of socio-economic disparity and of domination and subordination. They are very likely to oppose 'secularisation', and ignore the protection of the weak. They are likely to devise easy methods of forestalling conflicts and submerging tension from the society, without solving the basic problems involving change in the social structure.

A resort to emotionality and cultural revivalism as also the creation of a feeling of insecurity and fear psychosis are some of the methods applied for submerging tensions and creating cohesion, at least temporarily, in a strife torn society. Threat is visualised from an external common enemy, real or imaginary who has to be identified on the basis of cultural differences.

Thus conflicts and tensions in the hierarchically stratified caste society is not likely to remain confined to the society itself, but is also likely to extend to the communities outside the pail of the Verna-jati system. Such a community, with its significantly large numbers and with its conspicuous presence in the neighbourhood can serve as an easy 'scape-goat' towards which attention can be successfully diverted at least for sometime or occasionally, when situation demands. The attitude of a section of the dominant composed of system maintaining elites towards the numerically significant minority community is fully indicative of the point.

Antagonising the underprivileged, within the caste society, against the significant minority may be laboriously worked up through creation of myths, distortion or re-interpretation of historical events as well as cultural facts. It may be done through playing upon sentiments as well as through temptation to amass fortune at the cost of the vanquished adversary. The whole game may be politically motivated to gain support of the antagonised disappointed sections of the caste society for achieving power.

This may have its effect within the siginficant cultural minority namely the Muslims. They may close their ranks and forge unity to meet the challenge. The vested interest among them may seize the opportunity to keep them in dominating position at the cost of their own co-religionists. The behaviour of a section of the minority press and similar other institutions is indicative of the trend. Thus the problems of development, modernisation and social change in their society may recede to the background, and the exploitation of the underdog among them may continue.

The non-secular efforts laying stress on 'common culture' for the purpose of forging and restoring internal unity may be seen as designed to oppose democratisation and a redefinition of inter-relationship on the basis of the egalitarian norms of democracy. It has a retarding effect on efforts on the continuation and development of inter-community relationship on healthy lines, based on the model of two or three emerging classes on both sides of the community boundary, each coming closer to its counterpart on the other side of the community boundary. It may also retard the development of multiple cross-cutting relationship in the interest of broad based coherence.

The Problem

The interaction of the system of caste with the forces of modernisation in the sphere of inter-group relationship may normally be expected to result in the development of the secularisation of the society. This process is likely to lead to greater solidification or combination of a number of jatis within the system, approximating class divisions, though not of classes in the strict sense of the term, before achieving its ultimate goal of atomisation. The emerging groups of castes or jatis may progressively lose their passivity and confront each other in active competition.

Modernisation activities involving a rational approach to the problems of land reform, agrarian planning, rural development and political participation through adult franchise etc., are not likely to be smooth and lineal in nature, in a society cherishing a deep rooted tradition of institutionalised inequality. Since many of these activities involve redefinition of status and roles beyond the traditional pattern, as well as interaction across group boundaries on non-traditional lines, the process of change will imply multiple contradictions, tensions and even violent conflicts. The continuum model of social change will rather tend not only to be dialectical invloving conflicts but also digressions and diversions.

The formidable change in the traditionally passive caste society has larger implications on inter-community relationship particularly between Hindus and Muslims and this is the main focus of our study.

Thus it will be of interest to observe how some leaders or a reflective section of the traditional caste society react to the emergence of tension and conflict within their society and what solution is devised by them to forge unity or submerge tension in their conflict ridden society. How this situation is handled as an effective political weapon by a number of political parties having exclusive following?

It may also not be devoid of interest to observe the impact of the methods devised for the restoration of inter-jati cohesion on the Muslim Communities or ethnic groups. How do

Muslims react to the situation? Do they constitute a block in responding to the situation or their varied segments of different levels of social hierarchy align themselves or sympathise with specific jatis in their caste-cum-class struggle? The total impact of the situation on the Muslim community and their different segments may also be of interest to observe.

Methodology of Enquiry

This is basically a study of social structure as a system of social relations between the differentiated parts of segments of society in a state of transformation under the impact of new elements introduced as a result of induced change of very basic nature. This is required to be done through an attempt to describe observable empirical conditions. The study involves a simple and concrete definition of component parts in historical as well as in contemporary situations and their relations to each other as they are taking shape under the impact of induced change in the system. The component parts are castes or ethnic groups and their socio-economic strata as also their background, providing basis for their proximity or distance from each other and formation of class-like groupings. Connections among as well as within the parts has been presumed as social relation between people finding expression in communication. Yet another dimension of social relations between various segments of society has been supposed to be observed in attitude and behaviours of the people as verbalised and are observable.

Thus the relationship is required to be observed at two different levels viz. (1) actual relationship as it obtains in the functioning of the society and (2) the perception of each category about the nature of relationship with other categories.

The field methods applied include household census and socio-economic survey of selected villages, open ended and structured interviews as well as observation of behaviour in many relevent context. Documentary materials including newspaper reports were used. At the level of analysis endeavour has been made to co-relate the micro with the macro as far as practicable.

Area of Study

The area selected for the collection of data at the micro level are two villages in the Southern suburb of Bhagalpur city which is both the district and divisional headquarter. The villages namely Phulwaria and Jamgaon are at the distance of six and eight kilometres respectively from Bhagalpur city and are situated along Bhagalpur-Dumka road. The former having been in the erstwhile Zamindari of Brahmins and the latter under that of Muslims, provide the opportunity of comparing intra-village interaction patterns in the historical context. The two vlllages are adjacent to each other and each is multi-caste and multi-ethnic. The castes and ethnic groups present in these villages present in these villages represent all the strata of social hierarchy to provide the opportunity of observing the nature of their interaction.

In the chapters that follow we shall make an endeavour to describe the region and the villages and the people living in these villages and then proceed to observe the kind of inter-relationship that exists between them and is taking new shape. We shall then make an attempt to delineate the pattern of inter-relationship at inter-community level.

2

The Region

The district of Bhagalpur[1], where our field is situated, lies in the central part of the Bhagalpur division of the state of Bihar. It is situated between 86°30′ to 87°30′ longitude and 24°30′ to 25°30′ latitude. On the northern borders of Bhagalpur lie Saharsa, Purnea and Kathiar; on its southern and eastern borders are the districts of Sahebganj and Santhal Parganas, while the district of Munger is situated on its western borders. The Ganga flowing from west to east cuts Bhagalpur into two parts and separates north from the south. The bulk of the district is, however, in the southern part.

The northern part of the district is alluvial, while the southern part has two distinct physical features. The southern extremity bordering Santhal Pargana is upland, while the rest of the southern part is plain.

Besides the Ganga which flows from west to east, the district has another river Chanan which originates from south in the Santhal Parganas, north of Deoghar, and passing through Banka proceeds towards the Ganga. Its several distributaries rejoin the main stream to meet the Ganga at Ghogha, situated at a short distance, towards the east, from Bhagalpur city. The

1. Bhagalpur Dist. Census Hand-book, Census of India, 1981. Series 4, Part XIII, A & B.

district experiences an average rainfall of 1,174 mm, and has a hot summer from March to June, and a fairly cold, rather pleasant winter from November to February. The monsoon rain sets in mid-June and continues up to September.

Three small patches of forest in the district are situated in Banka, Baunsi and Katoria, which among others have *sal* and *mahua* trees as well as wild life like deer, barasingha and sambhar. The black faced monkey, locally known as 'hanuman', has in recent years grown out of proportion and has assumed a serious threat to horticulture and various other crops as well as to the tiled roofs of villager's huts. Besides the laws relating to the preservation of wild life in general and a hightened religious feeling among a section of the people, particularly the Ramayana serial on T.V. has made it very difficult for the people to deal with this menace, because this monkey is identified with Hanuman. The material loss to the people due to the deprada-tion of this black faced monkey is enormous.

The district of Bhagalpur consists of three sub-divisions namely Sadar, Banka and Naugachia. The first two sub-divisions viz. Sadar and Banka lie south of the Ganga and the last mentioned is situated towards the north of the river.

The district is divided into 21 Community Development Block-cum-Anchals of which 8 are situated in the Sadar sub-division, 10 in Banka sub-division and 3 in Naugachia sub-division. The villages from where we have drawn our data are situated in the Jagdishpur Block within the Sadar sub-division of the district. This block has 16 panchayats.

The southern part of the district is a distinct cultural and linguistic area like similar other areas of Maghai, Maithili, Bhojpuri, Jharkhand etc., in different parts of the state. The northern part comprising Naugachia has considerable influence of Maithili. The southern part may be identified with Anga and the dialect spoken in this part is known as Angika or Cheka-Cheki, as mentioned by Griarson in his book 'Linguistic Survey of India' Vol. V—Part II. It is this dialect that is spoken by the people of this area particularly the village folk. Edu-cated Hindus and Muslims endeavour to speak Hindi and Urdu respectively, which remain their respective forms of expression. Angika does not have its own script or any literary form of its own, though it is rich in oral folk literature. Both Hindus and Muslims have composed a number of poems in this dialect, which include religious themes. Angika has not achieved the level which Bhojpuri and Maithili have achieved in their respective area in the neighbourhood.

In recent years local radio-station has started presenting quite a few programmes, particularly for rural population in this dialect, which has tended to make Angika a little more popular and has given it considerable respectability.

Angika has had its impact on the Bhojpuri settlers in Bhagalpur who are from Shahabad and Balia, as also on Avadhi speakers who had migrated from Jaunpur during Muslim rule. Neither Awadhi settlers nor Bhojpuri migrants who had arrived in bulk around 1857 retain their original dialects and have adopted Angika as their own. Certain elements of Angika is, however, retained in the spoken language of upper class Muslims. At places where Bhojpuri settlers are in living contact with the area of their origin one may find traces of their dialect among them. The Maithili area is in closer proximity to the district particularly to its northern sub-division of Naugachi where its impact is observable.

Until 1870 Persian had been the court language when Sir George Campbell introduced Kaithi Hindi as an optional languge to be used in official transactions. In 1880 Kaithi, a special character, evolved by the Kayesthas, the scribe caste, replaced Persian. The vocabulary used in the court of official transactions, however, remained Persian, and this has remained unchanged until this day. The court documents fully use the Persian vocabulary, though it is generally written in Hindi or Devnagri script. Urdu or Persian script is also frequently used in these documents, particularly those presented for registration. Urdu has in recent years been accorded the status of second official language in the district, the impact of which is yet to be felt in any significant measure.

Bhagalpur's Historical Heritage: The district has a rich historical heritage going back to very ancient times. If the epics and the Puranas are included among the sources of history, they may seem as throwing considerable light on the region, though the information is very scanty and somewhat sketchy and occasionally misleading. It is gathered from these sources that the descendents of Anu, the great grandson of Manu, founded the Anava Kingdom in the eastern part of the sub-continent. This Kingdom was sub-divided into five parts, one of which was Anga, the present day Bhagalpur, named after one of Manu's sons.[2]

Again among the early rulers of Anga, a reference is stated to be to Lomapada, a contemporary of the king of Ayodhya. Lomapada's great grandson was Champa, after whom the capital of Anga was named. During the Mahabharata period, Anga was ruled by Karna, the eldest son of the Pandavas. Anga is stated to have been mentioned in Vedic literature, Atharvaveda Sampita.

Subsequent Buddhist literature mentions Anga among the different kingdoms of North India. There is a reference to a tradition that Brahmadutta, the king of Anga had vanquished Balliya, the king of Magadh, but the latters' successor Bimbisara (545 B.C.) avenged his father's defeat and subjugated Anga. Ajatshatru the next king of Magadh, is said to have transferred his capital to Champa, which had assumed the position of an important river port. It was from this port that merchant ships sailed down to the delta of the Ganga and further along the east coast of India to Southern Peninsular India. These ships used to bring back spices and precious stones which had added to the wealth and prosperity of the Magadh Empire. Both Buddha and Mahavira, the founders of Buddhism and Jainism lived in the reign of Bimbisara. Bimbisara's son Ajatshatru had starved his father to death and as a penance he got converted to Buddhism.

2. Bengal Dist. Gazette, Bhagalpur, J. Byrne. 1911.

Ajatshatru's grandson Udayin, built a new capital at Pataliputra. Asoka's mother Subhadrangi, a poor Brahmin girl, is said to belong to Champa.

Anga, having lost its independence to Bimbisara, remained a part of the Magadhan Empire under the successive dynasties of Nanda, the Maurias (324-185 B.C.), the Sisunga (185-75 B.C.) and the Kanvas (75-30 B.C.), It was during the rule of the Kanvas that King Kharavela of Kalinga invaded Magadh and Anga.

The subsequent history of Anga, for several hundred years is shrouded in darkness. It is, however, known that Anga was a part of the great Gupta Empire (320-455 A.D.). Until this period both Buddhism and Jainism had flourished in an unprecedented scale. Gupta period is a period of Hindu Renaissance or revival of Brahminism in India, involving revival of Sanskrit language, reinstallation of chief gods of the Hindu pantheon like Shiva, Vishnu and Brahma and overshadowing of Buddhist and folk culture and language by the elitist group. Brahmans were no longer on the retreat but came very much into their own, dominating the socio-cultural life.

The capital of the Gupta Empire was Patna and it was powerful enough to be acknowledged as supreme by the kings of different countries. The revival of Brahminism and consequent decline and retreat of Buddhism and Jainism was in proportion to the might and extent of the Empire.

The Gupta Empire was over-run by the Gauda King Sasanka in 602 A.D. who continued to rule over this area until 625 A.D. when he died. Anga again formed part of the Magadh empire under Harsha in 687 A.D. Sananka, a worshipper of Shiva was accused by Hiuan-Tsang of oppressing Buddhism and even cutting down the Bodhi tree and of making an abortive attempt to replace the image of the Buddha by an icon of Maheswara in the shrine near the Bodhi tree (Mukherjee, B N, with reference to Hai-yu-Chi, Chuan IV, V, VI I and VIII).[3]

3. B.N. Mukherjee, Tension & Tolerance in Pre-Islamic India. The Telegraph, Calcutta, 30.11.90.

It was in the 7th Century A.D. that the Chinese traveller Hiuen Tsang, after his term of years in the Buddhist monastry at Nalanda, travelled through south Bihar and visited Champa, the capital of Anga, the present day district of Bhagalpur. Anga was then under the rule of Khetauries of Mal origin and was at the time a powerful kingdom with its flourishing trade.

During the first half of the 9th Century the kings of Pala dynasty rose to power in the kingdom of Anga and extended their sway over Bihar and North Bengal. The Palas were Buddhists but were tolerant of Hinduism. They stemmed to some extent the setback to Buddhism which it had suffered right from the time the Guptas had assumed power. But the Pala kings soon yielded place to the Senas of Bengal who were again non-Buddhists. The Senas ruled over Anga right up to the dawn of the 13th Century A.D. when Bakhtiar Khilji annexed the kingdom to the Sultanate of Delhi.

It may be mentioned that right from the 8th Century A.D. a number of Rajput principalities had emerged and had set up new kingdoms in Northern India and in Deccan. Besides absolute rulership a king of feudal structure had emerged and sectarian Hinduism gained immense popularity under their patronage. These Rajput Kingdoms by and large pursued the policy of the Guptas from the 4th to the 7th. Century A.D. in re-establishing the superiority and dominance of the Brahmanical religion and suppressing or over-shadowing the common man's culture and language. There was a sharp decline of both Buddhism and Jainism.

Rajputs had great faith in the caste system which assumed new rigidity. The Brahmans were greatly respected and their cult and mode of worship gained tremendous popularity. Untouchability was strictly enforced. The religion of the Rajputs had no place for *Ahimsa* and human equality, the underlying principles of Buddhist and Jain religions. The impact of the emergence of sectarian Hinduism was all out and widespread. It was often aggressively imposed.

It is amusing that while the conflict between orthodox Hinduism on the one hand and Buddhism and Jainism on the other spread over centuries prior to the advent of the Muslims, have been very much underplayed, some historians particularly the British, attribute the decline of Buddhism in India to one incident of attack by Bakhtiar Khilji's forces on Nalanda, mistaken to be a fort. This mistake finds admission by the historians of the period. There is no evidence of Muslims attacking Vikramshila nor of the Muslim persecution of the Buddhist on ground of religion. Our Gazetteers and District Census Handbooks have almost ritually reproduced a statement published by its first British compiler,[4] that 'Bakhtiar Khilji sounded the death knell of Buddhism by trampling over Nalanda and Vikramshila'. History has a lot of indications to suggest that there has been a long period, spread over centuries, when Brahminism or sectarian Hinduism had been struggling, often violently, to gain supremacy over both Buddhism and Jainism which did not accept Brahman superiority. It was rather a period of reassertion of the system of caste, the superiority of which stood undermined by the teachings of both Buddhism and Jainism and Anga had not remained unaffected by the movement.

The long history of the Muslim rule, does not provide any evidence of Muslim rulers prosecuting either Buddhism or Jainism or even Hinduism. Far from demolishing temples and harassing priests, they are known to have given liberal grants of land to temples. By no stretch of imagination they can be considered to have destroyed any religion, though as rulers they had dealt rebellious forces with might, irrespective of the religion the rebels followed. The armed forces which were assigned the task of crushing rebellion or of conquest were often commanded by Hindu generals. The statement holding

4. J. Byrne, 1911, Bengal Dist. Gazetteer, Bhagalpur. This provides one of the numerous examples of the British rulers to blacken the image of the Muslims and to induce Hindu-Muslim conflicts. The incident has been quoted in Bhagalpur Dist. Gazetteer 1961 with further elaborations.

Muslim rulers responsible for sounding the death knell of Buddhism in Bihar is untrue and improper.

The long history of the successive rulers in Anga, roughly the present day Bhagalpur, brought with them waves of immigrants into the area, though immigration was into always linked with the advent of new rulers. The early settlers got acclimatised and absorbed in the socio-economic system, yet certain suffixes used by specific Hindu castes or their segments such as Kanojia, Maithil, Pachiara, Purabia, Tirthutia etc. give ample indication of the origin of these castes or their segments. The earlier immigrants have been linguistically absorbed in the area of their abode, the comparatively recent ones such as Bengalis or Marwaries who are either in living contact with their natal region or continue to pour in, have retained their language. This is also true of the Maithil and to a lesser degree of the Bhojpuri who are believed to have come in a large bulk around 1857.

A sizeable number of Bengali Hindu middle class settlers in Bhagalpur city owe their origin to the establishment of British rule. Being among the first to learn English they were called upon to serve the Government in various capacities in the administration, teaching, medical and engineering services and other white collar jobs which they monopolised or held in large numbers until independence. Bengali population continued to grow until the mid fifties. In 1961 the Bengali speaking population was 9048 mainly in the municipal areas of the Bhagalpur city. In 1981 they numbered 6,279 individuals. In recent years they no longer monopoly on the services, though some of their members are prominent among the political figures in the district. Mahashay Mahesh Ghosh, the well known water lord[5] and Vijay Kumar Mitra are among the leaders belonging to extreme rightist political parties.

The number of Marwari settlers has been on steady

5. The family holds the water lordship of the Ganga, with all its fishing rights, from Sultanganj to Perbainti.

increase. In 1951 Marwari population mainly concentrating in the city was 10,000 but it has since increased manifold. It is difficult to estimate the exact figure of the Marwaries since all of them have stated their mother tongue as Hindi in the Census reports. It is interesting that the census reports after 1951 have not recorded a single Marwari because the entire Marwari population has returned Hindi as their mother tongue, for reasons that are not difficult to understand.[6] Marwaris and Gujratis are mainly traders and they control almost the entire trade as well as the industries in the district and in the wake of growing resentment, against their near total control of the trade, among the newly emerging indigenous educated middle class, they have by and large adopted a political line of thought that supports extreme rightist ideology. A very effective control of trade and commerce in the district as also a systematic growth and expansion of the community in the numerical sense has given them confidence enough to involve themselves deeply in socio-political life and often take a leading role in various activities of the Hindu society. A good deal of patronage as well as leadership of Gao Raksha movement, the R.S.S., the newly formed B.J.P. and V.H.P. as well as Barjrang Dal comes from the Marwari community. In recent months a number of the members of the community pushed out of Assam due to movements led by AGP, ASU and particularly the ULFA, have arrived in Bhagalpur, after their role in helping ASU and AGP to divert their violent attitude towards Muslims did not produce lasting results. The instinct of self-preservation in the wake of a movement by a local youth organisation which had started raising slogans like "Marwari Hatao, Desh Bachao" a couple of years ago had alarmed the community and their role in the Bhagalpur riot of October 1989 is comprehensible for the purpose of Hindu unity for their own survival. Among the leaders who emerged at the time the names of Puran Mal

6. The population of the Marwaris in Bhagalpur according to a private census is stated to be above 25,000 individuals. The Jain of the Gujrati origin in Bhagalpur are about 2,000 individuals.

Bajoria and Shankar Lal Bajoria are mentioned among several others.

The Bengali Hindus and the Marwari and Gujrati live in the city along with a number of castes as well as Muslims. The Bhumihars, one of the forward castes, have systematically come to occupy a dominant position both in terms of number and socio-economic and political influence. Pushed by agrarian and law and order problems and pulled by an urge to benefit from facilities for education and opportunity for employment many a land owning rich people, mainly belonging to upper castes have shifted from the rural areas to the city. More significant among the new settlers besides the Bhumihar are Kanaujia Brahman and Maithil Brahman as also the Rajput. Attempts on the part of the indigenous people to relationalise the structure of opportunities in the scarcity ridden area have tended to create tension in the society involving either Bengalis or Marwaris. The movement led by the Kayasthas in the past decades under the slogan 'Bihar for Biharis'[7] and the students' movement that only a couple of years ago had raised the slogan "Marwari Hatao, Desh Bachao" are among the examples to this effect.

The Bengalis who once controlled the administration have yielded place considerably to local upper castes, as evidenced by their dwindling number. The Marwaries have grown from strength to strength, both in numerical and economic sense. However, traditionally both these communities have tended to solve the problem of adjustment with local people by laying emphasis on their Hindu identity in the multi-religious situation. This has frequently led to communalisation of the environment. The behaviour of the Marwaris is more significant in this respect whose 'communal exclusiveness' and 'patronage of Hindu revivalism' has been observed in Calcutta (Das : 1991 : 62).

7. N.K. Singh—"Many Faces of Caste Politics in Bihar", Economic and Political Weekly, April 8, 1972, p. 748.

Bhagalpur is among the most backward districts of Bihar, a state which is itself among the backward states in the country. Only 13.99% of the inhabited villages in the district are fortunate enough to be connected by one means of communication or the other.[8] The northern part of the district is still less fortunate in this respect. This is so despite the fact that almost entire district comprises plain areas, and it is relatively easy to construct roads and to make provision for other means of communication, 22.42% of the inhabited villages have been provided with electric connections, but power supply is extremely erratic and on an average not more than two hours in a day the power is available. This has resulted in the closure of 75 per cent of the small scale industries. The shortage continues for over two decades but the authorities have not succeeded in bringing about any improvement in the situation. The district gets power from Damodar Valley Corporation through one grid station at Sultanganj through a 132 KVA line. The five sub-stations supplying power to different areas are located at Barari, Aliganj, Amarpur, Banka and Kahalgaon.[8]

The literacy rate in the rural areas of Bhagalpur is 24.31% while in Bihar it is 26.20% and in India as a whole it is 36.23%. The female rate in Bhagalpur (13.62%) is again lowest in India excepting Rajasthan, the all India figure of the female literacy rate being 24·82%.[9]

In terms of urbanisation Bhagalpur may also be considered among the most backward districts of India. The percentage of urban population to total population in the district was 11·62 in 1981 which is even lower than the state average of 12·48 and far below the national average of 23.73%.[10] Considering the fact that a large segment of the urban

8. The Hindustan Times ; Patna, Dec. 1, 1987.
9. Census of India 1981, Series 4, Part IVA. Also Dist. Census Hand Book, Series 4, Part XIII A & B.
10. Bhagalpur Dist. Census Hand-book, Census of India 1981, Series 4 Part XIII A & B.

population in the district is not indigenous to the state and this segment is by and large in control of the urban economy, the problems of the people of the district become very much complicated. Thus urbanisation has had very little impact on the people of the district. In real sense Bhagalpur has been experiencing progressive ruralisation, a situation that compels people to depend more and more on agriculture.

The area of Bhagalpur has undergone frequency changes and as it stands today the district comprises an area of 5,589·00

TABLE 1

Percentage of Urban Population to Total Population in India and some States[11]

Sl. No.	*States*	*Percentage of urban population to total urban population* 1961	1971	1981
1.	Andhra Pradesh	17.74	19.35	23.25
2.	Bihar	8.43	10.04	12.46
3.	Gujarat	—	—	13.08
4.	Haryana	17.23	17.78	21.96
5.	Himachal Pradesh	6.34	7.06	7.72
6.	Karnataka	23.33	24.31	28.91
7.	Kerala	15.11	16.26	18.78
8.	Madhya Pradesh	14.29	16.26	20.31
9.	Maharashtra	28.22	31.20	35.03
10.	Nagaland	5.19	9.91	15.54
11.	Orissa	6.32	8.27	11.82
12.	Punjab	23.06	23.83	27.72
13.	Rajasthan	—	—	16.23
14.	Tamil Nadu	26.69	30.28	32.98
15.	Uttar Pradesh	12.85	14.00	18.01
16.	West Bengal	24.45	24.59	26.49
	All India	17.98	19.87	23.73

11. Vide Census of India 1961, 1971 and 1981.

TABLE 2

Showing the Growth of Population in Bhagalpur District (1872-1981)—unadjusted for change in territory which has undergone reduction with every change in area

Year	*Population*
1872	869,457
1881	967,278
1891	975,629
1901	1,018,743
1911	1,036,037
1921	966,645
1931	1,113,964
1941	1,273,061
1951	1,429,069
1961	1,711,136
1971	2,091,103
1981	2,621, 427

sq. kms. and a population of 2,621,427 individuals (1981 census). The district covers 3·21% of the states' land surface and accommodates 4% of its total population. It is thus one of the most densely populated districts of Bihar, a state which comprises 5.41% of Indias' land surface, but accommodates 10.50% of the country's total population. The density of population in the district in 1981 was 469 per sq. km. as compared to 402 per sq. km. in the state and 207 per sq. km. in India as a whole.[12]

A comparative picture of area, population and its density, male/female ratio, extent of urbanisation, literacy and other socioeconomic condition can be had from the following table.[13]

12. Bhagalpur Census Hand-Book, Census of India, 1981.
13. Based on the Census of India, 1981.

TABLE 3

S. No.	Particulars	India	Bihar	Bhagalpur	
1.	Total area in sq. km.	3,208,825	173, 877 (5.41 p.c.)	5,589 (3.21 pc)	Bihar 5.41 p.c. of India. Bhagalpur 3.21 p.c. of Bihar
2.	Population	665,287,849	69,914,734 (10.50 p.c.)	2,621,427 (3.74 p.c.)	Bihar 10.50 p. c. of India. Bhagalpur 3.74 p.c. of Bihar
3.	Population	207 per sq. km.	402 per sq. km.	469 per sq. km.	
4.	Male/Female ratio	—	1000; 946	1000:911	
5.	Urban Population	20.40 p.c.	12.47 p.c.	11.72 p.c.	
6.	Cultivators	13.90 p.c.	43.57 p.c.	38.56 p.c.	

7.	Agricultural Labour	8.34 p.c.	35.50 p.c.	41.42 p.c.
8.	Workers in Household Industry	1.15 p.c.	2.38 p.c.	4.78 p.c.
9.	Other Workers	10.03 p.c.	18.55 p.c.	15.24 p.c.
10.	Literacy	36.00 p.c,	26.20 p.c.	27.47 p.c.

This amply indicates the extent of backwardness of the district of Bhagalpur and the problems which its inhabitants are facing. The density of its population, next only to Kerala and West Bengal is alarming particularly when we see that over 80% of the population is dependent on agriculture.

The Economy

Bhagalpur is among the most economically backward district of a state which itself is known for its backwardness. The district lags behind both in industry and agriculture. It is a district within a state which is richest in India in terms of mineral resources as well as the fertility of its agricultural land but among the poorest in terms of per capita income. Bihar accounts for 40.57% of India's total mineral production e.g., coal, iron ore, limestone, mica, fire clay, copper, china clay and bauxite, 48% of coal and 100 per cent of iron ore is extracted from the mines in the state.[14] But in tcrms of urbanisation and industrialisation, the state lags far behind other states in India with much less resources.

The percentage of urban population in Bhagalpur is 11.72 even less than the state average of 12.46% and the national average of 23.73% Thus Bihar is about thrice as backward as Maharashtra (35.03%.), Tamil Nadu (32.98%) and Karnataka (23.91%) and about twice as backward as Andhra Pradesh (23.25%), Punjab (27.72%), West Bengal (26.49%) and Haryana (21.96%) in urbanisation. The percentage of urban population in Bhagalpur has been largely augmented by migrants from other states such as West Bengal, Rajasthan and Gujarat, who occupy important position in white collar jobs and in trade and commerce. The involvement of the indigenous population both in terms of quality and number in the city is insignificant.

14. Techno-Economic Survey of Bihar, Vol. 1, National Council of Applied Economic Research, New Delhi (Bombay, Asia Publishing House, 1956), pp. 5-8.

Industrially Bhagalpur has made very little headway. There is only one Industrial Estate in Bhagalpur located at Barari in Sabaur Block but, according to R.A. Chokhani, Secretary General of the Eastern Bihar Chamber of Commerce, out of 60 units in the Estate only five were functioning. The rest have become sick. Some small scale industrial units manufacturing steel trunks, furniture, industrial fasteners, cables, conductors, C.I. casting, leather shoes, soap and saline water, but none of these have been faring well. The cottage industries of blacksmith in Chanan and Katoria blocks have now become extinct.[15] The communal frenzy that overtook the city and the district from October 1989 to January 1990 has resulted in a large scale destruction of the cotton and silk textile cottage industry.

The agricultural land in Bhagalpur is among the most fertile in the country. But land reforms have left the district, like the whole of the state, largely unaffected. The four upper castes constituting a little over 10 per cent of the population of the district, control about 90% of the agricultural land. It is estimated that only two of the four forward castes, namely the Bhumihar and the Rajput constituting about 7% of the total population of the state own 78.6% of the land.[16] There is no wonder if the 1981 census reports indicate that while the all India figure of the landless agricultural labour is 8.34 per cent, it is 35.50% in Bihar and 41.42% in Bhagalpur.[17]

The percentage of cultivators, agriculturul labour, those engaged in household industry and other workers in the district have been shown in 1981 census reports as 38.56; 41.42; 4.78 and 15.24 respectively as compared to the corresponding state figure of 43.57; 34.50; 2.38 and 18.55.[18]

Over 80 percent of the total population of Bhagalpur depends upon the underdeveloped and outmoded agriculture.

15. Hindustan Times: Patna, Dec. 2, 1987.
16. N.K. Singh, "Many Faces of Caste Politics in Bihar", Economic and Political Weekly, Vol. 7 (15), April 8, 1972. p. 784.
17. Bhagalpur District Census Handbook, Census of India—1981.
18. Bhagalpur District Census Handbook, Census of India—1981.

Approximately 70% of the cultivators have uneconomic holdings and 41.42% are landless agricultural labour many of whom remain unemployed or underemployed. The extreme impoverishment of a very large section of the people can best be imagined.

Bhagalpur may appear to be fortunate in having 4.78% of its population engaged in household industries. The major household industry in the district is cotton and silk textile. But the supply of cotton and silk yarn as well as the marketing of the textile products is monopolised by the Marwari and the weavers have no control over the same. The system that operates does not allow the weavers to have their cooperatives either for the procurement of raw materials they need or the sale of their textile products, and it keeps them on the level of marginality.

Bhagalpur's journey, through history, from glory to degradation and from prosperity to impoverishment is instructive and thought provoking. The district had a glorious ancient as well as medieval past not only as a cultural centre but also as a centre of flourishing crafts and household industry of cotton and silk textiles. It has remained a major centre of commerce and trade.

Champa the ancient capital of Anga, the present day Bhagalpur was an important river port as early as several centuries before the birth of Christ during Ajatshatru's reign. The Chinese traveller Hiuen Tsang had visited Champa in the 7th Century A.D. He had found it a centre of flourishing trade and a powerful kingdom ruled by Khetauries.

The advent of the Muslims led to the building of new city of Bhagalpur adjacent to its previous capital and to its unprecedented expansion and development.[19] The resources of Bhagalpur were not plundered and carried elsewhere, they were spent on its development and glorification.

19. The names of the city's wards or mohallas such ss Shujaganj, Tatarpur, Mashaekh Chak, Mujahidpur, Mulla Chak, Aliganj, Mirjan Hat, Adampur, Sahebganj, Urdu Bazar, Khalifa Bagh, Mughalpura, Qutubganj, Kabirpur, Khanjarpur, Sarai etc.

The colonial rule set in the process of decay and impoverishment of its people. The Permanent Settlement of 1793 reduced the peasantry to serf. The industrial revolution in Britain dealt a mortal blow to its craftsmen. Instead of exporting their textile products, the people were made dependent on imported clothes and other articles. Since the people of the area where late in accepting westernisation and in acquiring English education, the people from the neighbouring state of Bengal came to serve in the administration, as technicians, as teachers, as doctors, lawyers and particularly in all Government activities. The Marwaris and Gujaratis came as traders and gradually occupied not only the central business district and central part of the city, but also almost the entire trade and commerce of the district and subjected the area and its craftsmn to worst kind of exploitation.

Though the British rule ended in 1947, Bihar never knew a break in the intensity of its colonial exploitation. As the role of the British capital declined, the Indian capitalists from outside Bihar jumped in the breach to continue the tradition of colonial loot.[20] (Upendra Mishra – 86 : 18).

Thus the economy of Bhagalpur, in the words of Dr. Sachidananda, who speaks of the whole of Bihar, can be aptly described to be from colonial status to colonial status.[21] The process of exploitation continues even after independence. The exploiting sections are so deeply entrenched into the socio-economic and political life of the distrsct, and have developed such a powerful network within and beyond the state that it is bound to be difficult to strike a balance in the society. The amount of power they yield and the nature of alliance they have made in the caste ridden society for their survival and continued dominance is indeed formidable and of far reaching consequences. It has direct bearing on inter-caste and inter-community relationship in the district.

20. Caste and Politics in India, 1986, p. 18.

21. Sachidananda Sinha, 1973. The Internal Colony: A Case Study in Reigonal Exploitation; Sandhu, Prakasan, p. 89.

3

The People

The society in Bhagalpur, as in other parts of Bihar, is segmented along religious, sectarian, dialectal, tribal and caste lines. Hindus constitute about 82.65 percent, Muslims 13.93 per cent and scheduled tribes 3.51 percent of the total population of the district. The population of the Christians, Jains and Sikhs is numerically insignificant and may be found only in urban areas. The population of the scheduled tribes is concentrated in the southern extremity of the district. Muslims and Hindus live side by side both in mixed and exclusive villages. The association of the Muslim population with the so called lower or backward and Harijan or Scheduled castes in the villages is more frequent that with the upper or forward castes, though their association with the latter is not altogether absent.

The Hindu society is highly stratified among caste lines. Caste serves as an important identity marker and people are more conscious of the caste they belong to and tee range of the kinship that operates in their society, than the village and the region they hail from. This means to say that ones' loyalty to caste and kinship, cutting across village boundaries, overrides his loyalties to the village he belongs to. Caste are hierarchically arranged with a clear notion of superiority and inferiority among

1. Census of India, 1931. Vol. VII ; Bihar and Orissa.

the caste in relation to each other. Castes are strictly endogamous and mobility of individuals from one caste to another is unthinkable. A system of functional interdependence or of receiving and rendering specialised services bind the various castes as also communities in a traditional system, though traditional occupations of rendering services are very small part of the total occupational pursuits.

The various castes in the Hindu society can be conveniently grouped into somewhat class-like categories of (i) upper or forward castes (ii) lower or backward castes and (iii) Harijans or scheduled castes. This categorisation has been found convenient for initiating welfare programmes and ameleorating measures by the state and several other social welfare organisations.

1. The upper or forward castes namely the Brahmans, the Bhumihar, the Rajput and the Kayastha all taken together contribute about 13.22 percent of the total population of the state. In the district their population is 10.66 percent.[2] Although the Brahmans are at the top of the hierarchy in the total caste system in the ritual sense, the four castes, despite their comparative numerical weakness, enjoy social prestige, economic power and are advanced educationally. They are in a position of dominance and are often referred to as *duijas* or twice born. These castes are the most privileged section of the society and occupy prominent position in economy, administration, bureaucracy and even in political leadership in the traditional sense. It is they who own agricultural land and in many ways exercise tremendous influence over various other segments of the population, particularly the backward and the scheduled castes.

A rough idea of the relative numerical strength of the four forward castes in Bihar may be had from the following table based on projection of 1931 census figures, because subsequent census reports do not provide separate figures relating to their population.

2. Vide 'Caste and Political Recruitment in Bihar' by Ramshray Roy in 'Caste in Indian Politics' Ed. : Rajni Kothari, New Delhi, 1970.

2. The lower or backward castes, traditionally known as the surdas are in fairly parse numbers such as the Bania, the Jadav, the Kurmi, the Koeri, the Barhai, the Dhanuk, the Kahar, the Kanu, the Kumhar, the Nai, the Tanti, the Mallah, the Lohar. the Teli etc. The backward castes may be grouped into two categories according to the degrees of their backwardness.

TABLE 4

Percentage Distribution of the four twice born (forward) castes in Bihar based on 1931 Census[3]

Castes	*Percentage to total population*
Brahman	4.76
Bhumihar	2.94
Rajput	4.26
Kayestha	1.26
Total	13.22

The Bania, the Jadav, the Kurmi, the Koeri are less backward and are often referred to as 'upper sudras', because they are economically more advanced, politically more conscious and assertive and numerically more significant, while the rest are grouped under the category of 'lower sudras' because of their comparatively more backward economic condition as also their numerical insignificance. The backward castes all taken together are majority and constitute 52.16 per cent of the total population of the state and 62.59 per cent of Bhagalpur's total population.

3. Census of India—1931. Vol. III, Part—II ; pp. 135-139.

An idea of the approximate relative strength of the various backward castes may be had from the following table based on the projection of 1931 census figures.[4]

TABLE 5

Percentage Distribution of Backward Castes in Bihar.

S. No.	*Castes*	*Percentage to total population*
1.	Bania	3.6
2.	Jadav	11.0
3.	Kurmi	3.6
4.	Koeri	4.1
5.	Barhai	1.0
6.	Dhanuk	1.8
7.	Kahar	1.7
8.	Kandu	1.6
9.	Lohar	1.3
10.	Kumhar	1.3
11.	Mallah	1.5
12.	Nai	1.4
13.	Tanti	1.6
14.	Teli	5.0
15.	Others	11.6
	Total	52.16

3. Harijan or Scheduled Castes, the so called untouchables are the most depressed section of the Hindu society. They cons-

4. The data is based on 1931 Census Figures, since separate population figures of individual castes do not appear in subsequent census reports. Census of India, 1931 ; Vol. III ; Part—III pp. 135-139.

titute 14.07 per cent of the total population of Bihar and 10.98 per cent of the total population of Bhagalpur, while the percentage of Scheduled Castes in the total Indian population according to 1981 census[5] is 15.74. They earn their living by scavanging, doing leather work, working as agricultural labourers, landless labourers and several other work considered degraded and unclean. According to the Government of India, Ministry of Home Affairs notification dated Oct. 29, 1956 and Scheduled Castes and Scheduled Tribes (Amendment) Act 1976 the following 23 castes have been listed as scheduled castes.[6] :

> Bantai, Bauri, Bhogta, Bhuia, Bhumij, Chamar, Chaupal, Dabgar, Dhobi, Dom or Dhangar, Dosadh or Dhari or Darhi, Ghasi, Halal Khor, Hari or Mehatar or Bhangi, Kanjar, Kurariar, Lal Begi, Musahar, Nat, Pan or Swasi, Pasi, Rajwar and Turi.

Being at the bottom of the hierarchy, in a state of extreme backwardness, the scheduled castes are subjected to exploitation not only by the forward castes but also by the backword castes as well. Separate population figures for each Scheduled Caste is not available but among them Chamar, Dosadh and Mushar are numerically important (Omvedt : 1982 : 103).

Scheduled Tribes. According to the Government of India, Ministry of Home Affairs notification dated October 29, 1956 and Scheduled Castes and Scheduled Tribes (Amendment) Act 1976 there are 29 individual tribes in the state constituting 8.31 per cent of the total population of Bhagalpur.[7] In Bhagalpur the Scheduled Tribes concentrate in the Banka Sub-division in the southern fringe of the district.

Muslims. Muslims are spread throughout the state where according to 1981 census they have a population of 9,874,933

5. Census of India, 1981. Series 4 ; Part IX.
6. Census of India, 1981. Bhagalpur Census Handbook, Series 4 ; Part XIII A & B. pp. 13-14.
7. The total population of the Scheduled Tribes in India is 51,628,733 constituting about 7.76 per cent of the total population of the country. Vide Census of India 1981, Series 4 ; Part IX.

out of a total of 69,823,154 individuals or 14.22 per cent of the total. In Bhaglpur,Muslims have a population of 365,313 constituting 13.94 per cent out of a total of 2,621,427.[8] Besides being divided on the basis of sects like Sunni and Shia they are segmented along beradaris either wedded to traditional occupations or having no traditional occupations. The latter include Syed, Sheikh, Mughal, Pathan and Mallick, while the former comprise a large number of groups having weaving, cotton carding, vegetable and fruit vanding, bangle selling, meat selling and a number of similar traditional occupations. These occupations were either pursued or have been abondoned but beradaris are based on these traditional occupations and are by and large endogamous, having their beradari panchayats at the local level to regulate their behaviour, which are either strong and effective or are weak and ineffective and on the wane. There is also an element of hierarchy in terms of social prestige, though in the sphere of religion no such hierarchy exists. The occupational groups of Muslims and Hindus serve both the communities indiscriminately and have a tradition of belonging to the jajmani system, purely on the local level, that includes Hindu Castes.

Table 6 based on 1931, 1951 and 1961 census may not give up to date figures of the population of the various segments of society, but it helps us in estimating the approximate relative strength of the population of the groups in the state. The districts in the state have undergone reorganisation since 1931. They numbered 30 in 1981. A subsequent change has also taken place and some more districts like Jahanabad and Sahebganj have been carved out of Gaya, Bhagalpur and Santhal Pargana respectively. However, figures with regard to the districts that have emerged later include in the original districts.

The relative numerical strength of the significant segments of the population namely the Forward or Upper Castes, the Backward or Lower Castes, the Harijans or Scheduled Castes, the Seheduled Tribes and the Muslims in Bihar as well as in

8. Census of India, 1981 ; Series 1 ; India, Paper 4 of 1984.

TABLE 6

Percentage Distribution of Castes and Communities by Districts in Bihar based on 1931, 1951 and 1961 Census report[9]

S. No.	*Districts*[10]	*Upper Castes*[11]	*Lower Castes*[12]	*Scheduled Castes*	*Scheduled Tribes*	*Muslims*
1.	Saran	22.65	55.02	10.33	—	12.00
2.	Champaran	11.79	57.75	14.56	00.10	15.80
3.	Muzaffarpur	16.84	59.57	14.89	—	8.70
4.	Darbhanga	15.80	56.33	14.67	—	13 20
5.	Saharsa	10.00	66.80	17.18	00.44	6.30
6.	Purnea	42.38	12.24	3.91	5.27	36.20
7.	Shahabad	26.59	49.81	16,01	00.69	6.90
8.	Patna	15.19	59.47	16.09	00.05	9.20
9.	Gaya	16 64	49.10	24.54	00.02	9.70

10.	Munger	21.28	53.23	15.81	1.38	8.30
11.	Bhagalpur	10.66	62.59	11.58	3.77	11.40
12.	Santhal Parganas	4.18	40.62	7.56	38.24	9.40
13.	Palaman	9.24	36.09	25.93	19.24	9.50
14.	Hazaribagh	7.03	58.12	15.55	11.30	11.00
15.	Ranchi	2.62	25.92	4.55	61.61	5.30
16.	Dhanbad	20.27	41.09	17.86	11.08	9.70
17.	Singhbhum	2.93	43.59	2.97	47.31	3.20
18.	All Bihar	13.22	52.16	14.07	9.05	11.50

9. Ref. 'Caste and Political Recruitment in Bihar' by Ramshray Roy in 'Caste in Indian Politics' Ed. Rajni Kothari; Orient Longman, New Delhi, 1970. Figure for upper castes projected from 1931 census caste figures. Figures for Scheduled Castes and Scheduled Tribes taken from Census of India 1961; Vol. VI, Bihar, Part—II—A; p. 353 and figures for Muslims are based on Census of India 1951; Vol. IV, Bihar.

10. Some of the districts have since been sub-divided, as a result total number of districts in Bihar were 31 in 1981 Some more districts have subsequently been created.

11. Upper Caste include Brahman, Bhumihar, Rajput & Kayastha.

12. Lower Castes include all the castes intermediary between the upper and the Schdeuled Castes.

TABLE 7

Distribution of Muslim Population and their Percentage to Total Population in the Districts of Bihar in 1981.[13]

S. No.	Districts	Total Population	Mustim Population	Percentage to Total
1.	Purnea	35,95,707	14,95,557	41.59
2.	Kathiar	14,28,622	5,27,379	36.92
3.	Darbhanga	20,08,193	4,32,751	21.55
4.	Paschim Champaran	79,72,610	3,87,243	19.63
5.	Sitamarhi	19,32,147	3,56,479	18.45
6.	Purba Champaran	24,25,501	4,27,081	17.61
7.	Siwan	17,78,930	2,94,796	16.57
8.	Santhal Pargana	37,17,528	6,11,367	16.45
9.	Madhubani	23,25,844	3,67,771	15.81
10.	Gopalganj	13,62,123	2,07,368	15.22
11,	Giridih	17,31,462	2,61,300	15.09
12.	Muzaffarpur	23,57,388	3,36,331	14.27
13.	Bhagalpur	26,21,427	3,65.313	13.94
14.	Saharsa	29,53,803	3,70,757	12.55
15.	Hazaribagh	21,98,310	2,69,658	12.27
16.	Dhanbad	21,15,010	2,57,411	12-17
17.	Begusarai	14,56,?43	1,75,713	12.07
18.	Nawada	10,99,177	1,24,906	11.36
19.	Palamau	19,17,528	2,13,421	11.13
20.	Gaya	31,34,175	3,28,015	10.47
21,	Samastipur	21,16,876	2,06,035	9.73
22.	Saran	23,84,322	2,01,224	9.65
23	Aurangabad	12,37,072	1,18,988	9.62
24.	Rohtas	23,66,325	2,17,741	9.20
25.	Vaishali	16,62,527	1,50,855	9.07
26.	Munger	33,15,427	2,82.724	8.53
27.	Nalanda	16,41,325	1,36 808	8.34
28,	Ranchi	30,70,432	2,38,879	7.78
29.	Patna	30,19,201	2,25,014	7.45
30.	Bhojpr	24,07.600	1,55,598	6.46
31.	All Bihar	6,99,14,734	98,74,993	14.12

13. Census of India 1981; Series I, India; Paper 3 of 1984.

Bhagalpur may be estimated from tables 4 to 7. Though all the castes and tribes listed in the schedule of Bihar are not present in Bhagalpur in significant number, we find adequate number of groups representing all the strata of population in the area of our study.

The groups constituting the population of the two villages, from which data has been drawn in considerable detail, namely 'P' and 'J' as we have named tham for the sake of convenience are (1) Kanyakubj Brahman, (2) Jadav, (3) Dhanuk, (4) Tanti, (5) Brahai, (6) Nonia, (7) Gaurhi or Gorhi (Mallah), (8) Barai, (9) Nai, (10) Dhobi, (11) Chamar (12) Paswan, (13) Dom and among the Muslims are (14) Ashraf Sheik, (15) Sheikh and (16) Mansoori. There is no group belonging to Scheduled Tribes in the villages.

Groups like (1) Kanyakubj or Kanaujia Brahman, (2) Dhanuk, (3) Brahai, (4) Chamar, (5) Dom and Muslim Mansoori are exclusive to Village 'P', while groups like (1) Ashraf Sheikh, (2) Gorhi, (3) Nonia, (4) Barai and (5) Dhobi are exclusive to Village 'J'. Groups like (1) Jadav, (2) Nai, (3) Tanti, (4) Paswan and the Muslim groups of (5) Sheikh are in both the villages. Thus altogether 16 groups representing Forward, Backward and Harijan castes and also various strata of Muslim society in thc region, constitute the population of the two contiguous villages of 'J' and 'P' selected for a considerable detailed study. Incidentally the two villages differ from each other in the respect that until 1962 when Zamindari system was finally abolished in Bihar, the former was under Muslim Zamindars while the latter was under that of the Kanyakubj Brahmans. Hindus constitute a majority in both the villages. Both the villages are contiguous to each other, and share identical natural and physical environment.

All the 16 castes and communities significantly grouped under Forward Caste (17.73%) Backward Castes (45.27%) Scheduled Castes (8.78%) and Muslim Ashraf (2.61%) and Non-Ashraf (25.59%) present an approximate proportion of each categories at the district as well as the state level, except that the proportions of Brahman and Muslim Non-Ashraf are a little higher than the average at the wider level.

TABLE 8

Showing Group Wise Distribution of Population in Village 'J' and Village 'P' respectively

S. No.	*Villages*	*Upper (Forward Caste)*		*Lower (Backward Caste)*		*Scheduled Caste*		*Muslim Ashraf*		*Muslim Non Ashraf*		*Total*	
		House Hold	*Population*	*House Hold*	*Population*	*House Hold*	*Population*	*House Hold*	*Population*	*House Hold*	*Population*	*House Hold*	*Population*
1.	Jamgaon	—	—	235	1290	28	145	24	118	86	376	373	1929
2.	Phulwari	99	802	140	754	60	252	—	—	161	781	460	2692
3.	Total	99	802 (17.73)	375	2944 (45.27)	88	397 (8.78)	24	118 (2.61)	247	1157 (25.59)	833	4521

Before making a detailed analysis of inter-relationship between these groups within the respective villages it will be appropriate to present brief exhnographic notes on each of the 16 ethnic groups or castes to have some idea of their backgrounds as well as the nature of their role in contemporary life.

(1) The Kanaujia or Kanyakubj Brahmans are one of the two major sections of Brahmans in Bhagalpur, the other section being Maithil. The Kanaujia and Maithil function as distinct caste groups, each being not only separately endogamous but also having their mutual relationship characterised by competition rather than co-operation, at least at the local level. They are observed having their separate localities or areas of residence in the village, due probably to food habits and respective corporate life, showing considerable exclusiveness in socio-religious matters. The Kanaujia are traditionally strict vegetarians while like the Brahmans of Bengal the Maithil consume certain non-vegetarian items of food. The Kanaujia Brahmans have a tradition of migration from Kanauj, the Maithil have migrated from areas north of the Ganga.

The Brahmans, both Kanaujia and Maithil, along with the Rajput, the Bhumihar and the Kayastha have socially, economically and politically been enjoying a traditionally dominant position and are much ahead of others. They are therefore known as a forward caste. In the area of our study the forward are represented by Kanaujia Brahmans only. Even among the forward group the Kanaujia being a priestly caste enjoy the highest ritual status in the total caste society in the region. They are traditionally placed at the highest position in the Verna order.

Besides being priests the Kanaujia are landholders, teachers, doctors, lawyers, engineers and businessmen. They serve the army and the air force, hold white collar jobs and are bureaucrats as also political leaders. Those who pursue agricultural occupation, engage labour for the purpose and avoid ploughing with their own hands. In recent years the educational advancement of the Kanaujia Brahman has been quite impressive.

The Kanaujia Brahman have no sub-caste, but are divided into exogamous gotras of Sandiliya, Vasta, Savarma, Kashyap, Bhardwaj, Kaushik, Matyana, Vasista, Garg, Pansar, Gautam etc. The surnames used by them are Pande, Dube or Dwivedi, Pathak, Upadhyay, Trivedi, Choube or Chaturvedi, Misra etc.

The Kanaujia Brahmans are generally monogamous but polygyny is allowed in their society. Divorce is not permitted. The system of dowry is among the major problems faced by the community. The status of women in their society is rather low and the male enjoy a dominating position. This may have a correlation with a peculiar demographic feature of their society indicating a very low proportion of the female (1000 : 782) in the village surveyed.

In Village 'P' out of a total of 460 households, there are 99 households of the Kanaujia Brahman with a total of 802 individuals comprising 352 female as against 450 males.

Family types among the Kanaujia Brahman are 40.4% nuclear, 38.3% extended, 12.2% joint, 2.02% nascent, 2.02% complex and 5.05% broken.

Over 85% of the Kanaujia Brahman households own agricultural land but very few are engaged in agricultural occupations. 13.0% are either landless or have small uneconomic holdings. Those of them who are agriculturists do not till the land themselves, they engage agricultural labour from amongst the lower castes in the village.

Out of a total of 166 working hands in the 99 households of the Kanaujia 93 are either in Government service or employed in organised sector or banks, 18 are in agricultural occupations, 19 in private service, 19 in petty business, 6 are motor drivers in the state or private buses or lorries and 3 are engaged in the traditional occupation of priests.

Illiteracy among the Kanaujia Brahman is very low (3.36%. Only old women come under this category of illiterates. 71.07% are educated and the rest are merely literate. The standard and quality of education received by the members of the community is decisively higher than those received by other communities.

(1) The Jadav also known as Ahir, Goala, Gope are a cattle rearing and dairy farming caste and are generally engaged in milk and curd business. They have also taken to agriculture. Jadav are traditionally vegetarians, though in recent years some of them have started taking non-vegetarian food, but not beef because the cow is an object of worship to them. The community is included in the list of 'Other Backward Castes' (OBC), for the purpose of ameleorating measures to uplift them.

The community is divided into the sub-castes of (i) Goria, (ii) Kanaujia, (iii) Kishnaut, (iv) Majraut, (v) Bandhor[14] and (vi) Bhumihar.[15] Of these six sub-castes only three viz. Goria, Majraut and Kishnaut are in the district of Bhagalpur while we find only Goria and Majraut in the area of our study. All these sub-groups are endogamous but in recent years cases of inter-group marriage, particularly between the Goria and the Majraut have occurred.

Kishnaut claims the highest status on account of the belief that Lord Krishna was born into the group. Among the Goria and the Majraut, the latter claim higher status because unlike some members of the Goria sub-caste, they have not degraded themselves by making butter, a practice said to have been disapproved in Hindu scriptures.[16]

The Jadavs are by and large monogamous though polygyny is allowed in their society. Divorce is seldom practised, Widow or widower remarriage can take place. Only male children get share in father's property, women have a low status in the family and generally have little say in decision making at the family level.

Jadav households are present in both the villages of 'J' (60) and 'P' (18). 56.64% of the total number of families in both the villages are nuclear, 24.35 % are extended, 10.25%

14 & 15. These two groups have been mentioned in the report of S.B. Roy on People of India (unpublished).

16. H.H. Risley-'Tribes and Castes of Bengal', (1st. Ed. Calcutta—1981), pp. 282-286.

are complex and the rest are of incomplete, nascent and broken types.

In Village 'J', a village under the former Muslim Zamindari, the Jadav are comparatively better off due to substantial land transfers from the former land owners. As a result about 26% of the total number of workers are cultivators—14.10% are day labourers, 9.40% are bidi rollers, 3.50% are motor drivers, 15.30 p.c. are dairy farmers, 21.17 p.c. are serving in Government or organised sector including banks, 5.88% in private service and 5.88% in petty business. The percentage of landless among them is 15.00%

In Village 'P', a village under the former Zamindari of the Kanaujia Brahmans, 100% of the Jadav are landless. 47.82% of the total number of working hands in the community is daily wage earners, 13.01% are bonded labour, 8.69% are masons, 8.69% are dairy farmers, 8.69% are in private service, 4.35% are share-croppers and 8.69% do casual work.

The percentage of illiteracy at Village 'J' and 'P' is 49.86 and 75.82 respectively. Similarly the percentage of educated in the community in the two respective villages is 24.28 and 5.49. The Jadavs at Village 'J' far supersede their counterpart in Village 'P' in the standard and quality of education.

The Jadavs as a community are politically conscious and fairly assertive often to the extent of militancy. They have good number of leaders both at the local and the regional level. Their representation in the panchayat, state legislature and Parliament has systematically increased and is fairly impressive.

3. The Dhanuk are a fairly numerous caste and like the Jadav are listed as backward caste. They are regarded as clean Sudras, who previously served mainly as domestic aids of the higher castes. They are reported to be slaves in the past who have freed themselves to a large extent.[17] Some of them, both men and women serve as domestic servants in the house of

17. H.H. Risley: 'Tribes and Castes of Bengal' (Ist. Ed. 1891), Vol. 1, Calcutta - 1981; pp. 220-222.

Brahmans. They are generally poor and landless, working as agricultural labour, casual labour and occasionally as share-croppers.

According to Risley (1891) the Dhanuks are divided into a number of sub-castes or exagamous clans such as (1) Tirhutia, (2) Kanaujia, (3) Maghaiya, (4) Avadhia, (5) Chhilatia, (6) Saukatwa, (7) Nageswar, (8) Sonpuri, (9) Sunri, (10) Jaiswar, (11) Kathautia, (12) Dojwar etc. In the area of our study we come across Kanaujia and Tirhutia sub-castes only. They are an endogamous community practising exogamy at the sub-caste level.

Dhanuks are present only in Village 'P' where they have 35 households, with a total population of 175 individuals, 86 male and 89 female. The average family size is 5.00 and a unique demographic feature of female numerically superseding the male, the ratio being 1000 : 1004. The main family types are Nuclear (57.14%), Extended 17.14%), Joint (8.57%), Nascent (5.71%) and Broken (11.42%) Dhanuks use Mondal and Roy as their surname.

The Dhanuks are generally monogamous but polygyny is allowed in their society without any restriction on the number of wives. Divorce is not permitted but a widowed woman is free to marry anyone she likes.

All Dhanuk are landless. Out of a total of 42 working hands 23 (54.76%) are daily wage earners, 3 (7.14%) are rickshaw pullers, 11 (26.19%) are in private service, 2 (4.76%) are low grade employee of the Government, 1 (2 39%) work as mason and 1 (2.38% is in petty business.

58.26% of the Dhanuk are illiterate, 10.85% have received low level of education and the rest are just literates.

4. The Tanti are another caste included in the list of backward classes (OBC). They are more depressed than the Jadav and the Dhanuk. Having largely abandoned their traditional occupation of weaving and being landless they are engaged as day labourers or in marginal occupations of bidi rolling and similar other work. The ritual status of the Tanti is

rather low. They occupy a status below the Jadav, Dhanuk, Gorhi, Nonia and Nai, and accept kacha and pucca food from all these castes.

Tanti have various divisions or sub-castes such as Kanaujia, Tirhutia, Baiswara, Uttarana etc. These are of endogamous character. Totemic clans of Nag, Sal, Kashyap etc. are exegamous. Polygyny is allowed and divorce is permissible in their society. Widow or widower remarriage takes place. Traditionally bride price was in vogue but the system of dowry is gasning ground.

The Tanti are present in both the Villages selected for observation, 122 households in Village 'J' and 65 households in Village 'P'. 55.08% of the total number of families in both the villages are of nuclear type, 26.73% are extended, 2.13% are joint and 4.81% are of the broken type. Complex and nascent types of families also come across. The average family size of the total Tanti population is 5.02 and male/female ratio is 1000 : 865.

91.50 per cent of the Tanti have either no land or merely small holdings barely sufficient to build their huts. A few have kitchen garden as well. 8.50% are small or medium cultivators.

At village 'J' out of a total of 174 working hands among the Tanti, 46 are daily wage earners, 85 are bidi rollers, 3 are mason, 4 are motor drivers, 12 are cultivators, one is dairy farmer, 4 are in private service, 3 are motor mechanics, 12 are engaged in petty business and 4 are casual labourers.

At Village 'P' out of a total of 85 working hands, 50 are daily wage earners, 1 is rickshaw puller, 8 are bidi roller, 3 are masons, 2 are motor drivers, 4 are share croppers, 3 are low grade employee of the Government, 4 are in private service, 3 are in petty business, 2 are casual workers and 5 are bonded labour.

The percentage of illiteracy among the Tanti at Village 'J' is 58.79 while at Village 'P' it is 76.94. About 11.00% in both the villages have received some sort of education. The percentages of literacy in the community at Village 'J' and 'P' are 31.10% and 12.06% respectively.

5. The Barhai or carpenter are an artisan caste claiming descent from Viswakarma and have close affinity with Lohar or ironsmith. They are also included in the 'OBC' list and are treated as clean Sudras. They use Sharma as their Surname.

The Barhai have several sub-divisions such as Maghaia, Mathurai, Kakas, Lohar etc. based eilher on territorial affiliations or the nature of occupation pursued. Clans like Kashyap and Bhardwaj are of exogamous character, while the community as a whole is endogamous. Barhai are generally monogamous but polygyny is permissible. Divorce from either side can take place usually on grounds considered valid by the society. Remarriage of the widow, widower and the divorcee is allowed. Marriage with the deceased wives younger sister and elder brother's widow is permissible in their society.

Barhai are settled only in Village 'P', where they have 9 households with 55 individuals, 33 male and 22 female, the average family size being 6.11. Five (55 00%) of the families are of the nuclear type, two (22.00%) are extended and two (22.00%) are incomplete in the sense that the spouse do not have children. Six (66.66%) of the households are landless, two (22.22%) have small uneconomic holdings and one (11.11%) is a small farmer.

All the nine households are engaged in carpentry works, mainly as wage earners. Since the daily wage of a carpenter is more than double of the wage of an unskilled labour, the Barhai are better off than other 'backward' communities in their neighbourhood.

Percentage of illiteracy among the Barhai is 40 while 47.27% have acquired education at least up to a low level. In recent years quite a few Barhai youth have received college education.

6. The Nonia or Nonhar are another caste listed as 'OBC'. They have a traditional occupation of making salt and saltpetre, and are ranked as Sudra in the Verna order. Locally they have lower status than the Jadav but higher than the Tanti.

Besides Bhagalpur, the population of the Nonia is distributed in Begusarai, Darbhanga, Muzaffarpur, Samastipur, Saran and East and West Champaran districts. Territorial divisions such as Awadhia, Bhojpuria, Maghaia and Pachiara characterise the Nonia society. Also divisions like Kharaut and Been Bind are also reported to be present among them. Risley (1891) mentions such divisions also as Chouhan and Simarwar among the group as also Gotras like Sankh and Kashyap of exogamous character.[18]

There is a notion of hierarchy among these divisions and Awadhia claim precedence over all others. In Bhagalpur Nonia use Mahto and Mandal as their surname. The caste is endogamous but the gotras and lineages are exogamous.

Nonias are generally monogamous, though polygyny is permitted in their society. Divorce may be resorted to from either side. Remarriage of widow, widower and divorcee can take place. Elder brother's widow and deceased wife's younger sister can be married. Dowry is in vogue. Inheritance of property follows the rule of male equigeniture and daughters do not inherit property.

The traditional occupation of the Nonia of making salt and saltpetre had a serious setback when the British started importing pottasium nitrate. A number of them continued to pursue this occupation until the first quarter of the present century, but they had to abandon this when it became utterly uneconomic. They took other occupation such as daily wage earning, agricultural labour and that of small farmers.

Nonia are settled in Village 'J' where they have 27 households with 178 individuals, 96 male and 82 female, average size of the household being 6.59 and male/female ratio being 1000 : 854. Family types are 55.50% nuclear, 29.62% extended, 7.40% complex, nascent and incomplete types are 3.70% each.

37.03% of the Nonia are landless, 21.00% have small

18. H.H. Rislay: 'Tribes and Castes of Bengal', (1st. Ed. 1891), Vol. I, Calcutta 1891; pp. 135.

uneconomic holdings and a little over 37.00% have land ranging from 2 to 10 bighas which they have largely acquired from Sheikh Ashraf co-villagers.

Of the 36 working hands 8.33% are daily wage earners, 2.73% are rickshaw pullers, 50.00% are bidi rollers, 2.78 are motor drivers, 8 33% are cultivators, 2.78% are in Government service, 5.50% are in private service and 19.40% are in business At least one family is involved in clandestime money lending business.

Percentage of illiteracy among the Nonia is 49.85% and 25.28% are educated. The rest are just literate.

7. The Gorhi or Gaurhi or Mallah are a fishing caste, probably originating from some aboriginal tribe. They are a backward community and have been listed with 'OBC'. They occupy a low position in the Verna order and Brahman do not accept water from their hands. Maithil Brahman priests preside over their life cycle rituals. The Gaurhi are also known as Mahaldar and use Mondal and Singh as their surname.

The community is divided into a number of endogamous sub-castes[19] such as Kolh. Banpar, Chab or Chabi, Dhoar, Kurin, Parbatti, Khunaut or Khulaut and Semai (Risley 1891). Though the Gaurhi are generally monogamous, polygyngy is allowed in their society. Divorce is also permitted and widow, widower and divorcee remarriage can take place. Marriage with deceased wife's younger sister and elder brother's widow is also permissible.

The Gaurhi catch as well as sell fish in the market. They also sell popped corn and parched grain in village markets and are generally better off as compared to other backward castes in the neighbourhood.

The Gaurhi are generally Vaishnavites and Panchpiria. There is also some influence of Kabirpanthi sect upon them.

In the area of our observation they are found settled only at Village 'J' where they have 17 households with 98 individuals,

19. H.H. Risley : 'Tribes and Castes of Bengal' 1891. Vol. I, reprinted in 19?1 : Calcutta.

50 male and 48 female, average family size being 5.76, and male/female ratio being 1000 : 960. Family types among the Gaurhi are nuclear 23.52%, extended 52.34%, incomplete 5.88%, and broken 17.64% The Gaurhi are not a land owning community but 88.00% own very small holdings barely sufficient to build homestead. The rest do small farming which is their secondary occupation. Out of a total number of 35 working hands 74.00% are small traders, 6.14% are in private service, 5.71% are daily wage earners and 2.85% are rick-shaw pullers.

The incidence of literacy among the Gaurhi is 50.0% 24.48% have received some kind of education. The rest are just literates.

8. The Barai are a betel leaf growing community widely distributed in Bengal, Bihar and Uttar Pradesh. In Bihar their concentration lies in Samastipur, Madhubani, Darbhanga, Muzaffarpur, Begusarai and Bhagalpur.[20] Their population is largely found in the Gangetic plain, in areas where the climate is moderate with low humidity and medium rainfall, and is suitable for betel leaf cultivation. Members of the community also sell betel leaf and readymade pan, in shops and on market days.

The Barai are a backward community included in the 'OBC' list, thouah they have higher status among the backward communities. They are place among the Vaishya in the Hindu Verna systems and Brahmans are said to be accepting water from their hands. Risley (1891) mentions five sub-groups namely Chourasia, Jaiswar, Maghaia, Semaria and Sokhwa among the Barai. Such divisions as Purabia and Pachiara are also come across among the Barai. All Barai claim to belong to one gotra namely Kashyap and such surnames as Modi, Chourasia, Bhagat and Mehto are come across.

The chief deity of the Barai is Sokha which is worshipped by the community elder serving as priest. At all places where

20. S.N. Mhato : The Barai of Bihar : People of India ; (unpublished).

betal leaf cultivation is done there is Adi Sakti Mandir and this also is worshipped by a senior member of the community.

Barai society also allows polygyny though monogamy is the common practice. Divorce is also allowed by either side and remarriage of widow, widower and divorce is permitted. Marriage with elder brother's widow and deceased wife's younger sister is permissible.

Barai are only in village 'J' where they have only two households with 14 individuals, 8 male and 6 female. Both the families are of nuclear type. They are landless aud are engaged in selling pan in the bi-weekly market which is the only source of their livelihood. There is no pan cultivation in the village. Illiteracy is 22.42% and the rest are just literates. One of the households is Kabirpanthi, a sect that cuts across caste and communities in the area.

9. The Nai or Hajjam are another backward caste, included in the 'OBC' list. They are distributed throughout the state in almost all the villages. They do not only do hair cutting and shaving but also perform certain functions on the occasion of marriage in the family of their patrons and often serve as messengers.

The Nai have four divisions in Biharnamely Awadhia, Kanaujia Maghaia and Tirhutia, all based on the area of their origin. These groups are of endogamous character. Gotras do not exist and lineages are of exogamous character. The Nai are monogamous but in case of chromic illness or barrenness of the first wife, a second one can be taken. Divorce though permissible is rare. Remarriage of widow, widower and divorce is permissible in the society. Marriage with elder brother's widow and deceased wife's younger sister takes place. Inheritance of property is according to the rules of male equigeniture. Female can inherit when there is no male sibling.

Twenty households of Tirhutia Nai are present in both the villages of 'J' (7) and 'P' (13), with a total population of 113 individuals, 62 male and 51 female. The average household size being 5.60 and male female ratio being 1000 : 822. Family types among the Nai is nuclear (60.00%), extended (15.00%) joint (10.00%), nascent (10.00%) and broken (5.00%).

At Village 'P' 9 out of 13 households (71.00%) are landless, the rest have small uneconomic holdings. At Village 'J' all the seven households possess small uneconomic holdings. Out of a total of 22 working hands in the community in both the villages 18.18% are daily wage earners, 9 09% are rickshaw pullers, 9.09% are sharecroppers, 4.54% are cultivators, 22.72% are low grade employee of the Government and 36.36% pursue their traditional occupation of hair cutting.

61.93% of the combined population of the Nai of the two villages are illiterate and 10.00% have received education of low standard while the rest are merely literate.

10. The Dhobi or washermen who are accorded a low status in society are a scheduled caste. Risley (1891) quoting Nesfield opines that the Dhobi have originally sprung up from the Bhangi, a scavanging caste of so called untouchables but have higher status than the Dom and the Bhangi.

Risley (1891) mentions such divisions of the Dhobi as Kanaujia, Maghaiya, Belwar, Awadhia, Batham, Gorsar, Gadhaiya, and Bangia.[21] Obviously most of these divisions are based on the areas of arigin. The Gadhaiya are those who keep ass for carrying bundles of cloth to the washing ghats. Such surnames as Baitha, Prasad and Rajak are used. The divisions, territorial or otherwise are endogamous. Marriage is regulated on the basis of lineages.

The Dhobi are monogamous but a second wife can be taken in the event of the barenness of the first. Divorce is permitted from either side and remarriage of widow, widower and divorce is also allowed. Daughters do not inherit property, the status of women is low but they are assets to the family.

There are 9 households of the Dhobi in Village 'J' having 50 individuals, 29 male and 21 female. The average size of the family is 5.55 and male/female ratio comes to 1000 : 734. 44.44% of the families are of nuclear type. 30.33% are extended, 10.00% are nascent and joint types respectively.

21. Vide H.H. Risley : 'Tribes and Castes of Bengal' Vol. I, reprinted in 1981. Pg. 223—236.

55.55% are landless and 44.45% have small holdings for cultivation. 44.45% depend on traditional occupation of washing clothes, 44.45% are serving Government or employed in the organised sector. 22.23% are cultivators and 11.22% are day labourers.

The percentage of illiteracy among the Dhobi is 28 while 48.00% are moderately educated. The rest are merely literate.

Dhobi have a caste panchayat, both at the local and regional level. They are conscious of the benefits the Government offers them as a scheduled caste and have considerably benefitted by these.

11. The Chamar or Charmakar, the leather working community are another group listed as scheduled caste. Their traditional occupation includes removal of carcass of the dead animals from the village, making and mending of shoes and working in tanneries. They are also drummers and musicians and their women serve as midwives, often without modern training. Chamars are untouchables for Hindu Castes, often their settlements are at considerable distance from the areas of residence of the upper castes.

According to Risley (1891) the Chamar have such sections as Dhusia, Dharh, Dohar, Khati-Mahara, Larkor, Janakpuri, Maghai and Pachiara.[22] The last four are obviously based on the areas of origin, others may indicate their ethnic origin.

Endogamy is practised at community level but no consanguinity is allowed. Monogamy is normally practised but polygyny is permitted. Divorce may take place from either side and widow, widower and divorcee remarriage can take place. Traditionally no purohit is engaged to perform their life-cycle ritual. Ceremonies are directed by the elders of the caste.

All the 30 households of the Chamars in the area of our study are in Village 'P' where their hamlet is at considerable distance from those of the upper castes. Their total population comprises 128 individuals, equally divided into male and female

22. H.H. Risley : 'Tribes and Castes of Bengal'. Vol. I, reprinted in 1981, Calcutta.

(1000 : 1000) and average size of the family is 4.16. 70 per cent of the families are of nuclear type, 13.33% are extended, 10.00% are incomplete and 2.66% are of the broken type.

97% of the Chamars are landless and out of a total of 32 working hands 18 are rickshaw pullers, 5 are daily wage earners, 2 are share croppers, 1 is in Government service (Police constable) as well as does cultivation, 2 are in private service, 1 is a shoemaker and 2 are bonded labour.

86% of the Chamar are illiterate and 8.59% have received education somewhat beyond the primary level. These mainly constitute school going children. The rest are just literate.

12. Paswan or Dosadh, as they are generally called, are another scheduled caste treated as untouchables in the Hindu Society. Criminality that was attributed to them in the past may not be true today, but because of the practice of pig rearing and pork eating they are accorded a very low status in the Hindu society. Members of this caste have traditionally been village watchmen or choukidars and village messengers. They are also cultivators and agricultural labourers.

The caste as reported by Risley (1891) has been assimilative, accepting members from other Hindu castes, except the Dom, the Dhobi and the Chamar, into their fold after a feast of pork and liquor.[23]

The Dosadh, according to Risley (1891) are divided into eight sub-castes (i) Kanaujia, (ii) Maghaia, (iii) Bhojpuria, (iv) Pailwar, (vi) (v) Kamar, Kuri or Kurin, (vii) Dharhi and (viii) Silkotia.[24] These are all of endogamous character and do not intermarry. They avoid consanguinity, Polygyny is permitted so is remarriage of widow, widower and divorcee. Elder brother's widow and deceased wife's younger sister can be married. Like the Chamar the Dosadh are not served by Brahman priests. Only degraded Brahmans are engaged by a few well-to-do Dosadh.

23. Vide H.H. Risley : Tribes and Castes of Bengal'. Vol. I, Reprinted in 1981, Calcutta pp. 252-258.

24. Ibid.

43 households of Dosadh are settled in the two villages under survey, 19 in village 'J' and 24 in Village 'P', with a total population of 193 individuals, 109 male and 84 female. The average size of the family is 4.07 and the male/female ratio is 1000 : 770. 41.86% of the families are of the nuclear type, 25.38% are extended, 6.97% are incomplete, 4.65% are complex and 16.28% are broken.

All the 24 households of the Dosadh at Village 'P' are landless while 73.68% at Village 'J' are landless and only 26% have small uneconomic holdings to cultivate. Of a total of 30 working hands at Village 'J' 5 (16.66%) are daily wage earners, 1 (3.33%) is rickshaw puller, 14 (46.66%) are bidi rollers, 1 (3.33%) is a mason, 5 (16.65%) are lower grade employee of the Government, 1 (3.33%) is engaged in private service and 3 (10.00%) are doing petty business.

At Village 'P' out of a total of 25 working hands 72% are daily wage earners, 12.00% are lower grade employee of the Government, 12.00% are in private service and 1 (4.00%) is a chowkidar.

63.24% of the combined population of the Dosadh in both the villages is illiterate. 14.07% have received low level of education not beyond high school standard and the rest are just literate.

13. The Dom or Bhangi are lowest of the groups in the Hindu society and are listed with Scheduled Castes. There are various divisions among the Dom, namely Bansphor, Bansmalik or Mughaia and Leder.[25] The Bansphor are basket makers, while the other two groups do scavanging work and are treated lower than the first. In social esteem the scavanging castes are lowest of the lowly.

Normally the three groups of the Dom are separately endogamous but there is considerable laxity in the choice of mate from other sub-groups. Monogamy is the common practice but the society is not opposed to polygyny. Divorce

25. B.K. Basu: 'The Dom', report on People of India, Anthropological Survey of India, (Unpublished).

as well as widow, windower and divorcee remarrige is permitted. Women do not have inferior status in society, though they do not inherit property.

Six households of the Dom are settled on the outer fringe of the main settlement in Village 'P' at considerable distance from the settlements of other groups, having a total population of 26 individuals, 17 male and 9 female. The average family size is 4.33. The male/female ratio being 1000 : 529. 66.66% of the families are of the nuclear type and the extended and the nascent types are 16.66% each. All the six households are landless, having no land of their own to build their huts upon. They are squatters on the road-side on the public land which has not been allotted to them.

These Doms belong to Maghaia sub-division and are mainly employed in hospital in the nearby town and under Municipal Corporation as safai-walas and are economically better off in comparison with other scheduled castes in the area. Only one of the seven working hands in the community is a daily wage earner.

It is interesting that the rate of illiteracy among the Dom is rather low. 30.76% of the members of the community are illiterate while 34.61% have received some sort of education or are in the process of receiving education in schools, the rest are merely literate.

14. The Ashraf (Sheikh) are one of the three Muslim beradaries or groups in the area of our study, the other two being the Sheikh (non-Ashraf) and the Mansoori or Cotton Carders. Socially the Ashraf Sheikh are a sharply segmented community having diverse sub-groups based on descent as well as sectarian affiliations.

Traditionally the Ashraf enjoyed prestige and social precedence over all other ethnic groups or beradaries within the Muslim community in the regional social framework, both on account of their origin or descent as well as due to their socio-economic condition, particularly educational status and a background of land ownership.

All the factors behind the prestigious position of the

Ashraf, except probably descent, have systematically corroded since the struggle of 1857 and they had continued to be downwardly mobile until the dawn of the current century in the area of our study. The pace of decline of the community was considerably stemmed under the influence of the Aligarh movement when the members of the community accepted modern education. But this proved transient and the decline set in sharply since the socio-political change after Independence, so much so, that their roots in the village have been rudely shaken. Many of their members have migrated to distant cities and even outside the country in search of livelihood. Their locality in the village gives a picture of desolation and their houses, with a few exceptions, are in a state of dilapidation and decay.

The small community of Ashraf, consisting of 24 households, a few of whom are only seasonally or occasionally present in the village, are sub-divided into various segments, based on (1) descent-cum-status and (2) sects.

1. The first segment consisting of descent-cum-status groups is sub-divided into two distinct categories :

(a) those who are born of both Ashraf parents and (b) those who are born of Ashraf father and non-Ashraf mother. The two groups are socially distinct from each other. The former enjoys higher prestige and does not normally establish matrimonial relationship with the latter, though the latter has started using the surname of the former. These two groups are associated in the same neighbourhood and have commensal and other relationships, though they have developed distinct kinship networks.

(a) The Ashraf of the first category in the village consist of several lineages interlocked with each other through marriage. Some of the lineages are original to the village while others are affinals and have settled in the village permanently for generations in a manner that distinction between the two categories no longer exists.

The history of the lineage original to the village goes back to about four centuries ago when its early ancestor belonging to Naqsh-bandia mystic order, with its centre at Sirhind,[26] Punjab, came on an assignment of chief Qazi of the district. It was a descendant of this family that participated in the struggle of 1857,[27] under the inspiration of Syed Ahmad Shaheed,[28] and had to undergo terrible sufferings. This category of Ashraf have had wider network of kinship incorporating not only the neighbouring districts but sometimes going beyond the boundaries of the state.

(b) The second category within this segment have traditionally been as an appendage to the first but since the socio-economic condition of the former does not justify the continuation of earlier relationship, they have a life of their own. Some among them have advanced educationally and have improved their economic condition while some others have degraded themselves and have established matrimonial relationship with members of non-Ashraf groups.

2. Segmentation on the basis of sects is a general characteristic of the Ashraf not only in the area of our observation but elsewhere too. In the village 'J' we have only two main segments of this kind, (1) the Sunni and (2) the Ahmadia popularly known as Qadiani. Elsewhere there is a good deal of controversy with regard to the position of the Ahmadia vis-a-vis the Muslim Society, but in Jamgaon no controversy of this kind comes to the surface nor there is any barrier to their intimate contact, though intermarriages do not take place.

Out of a total of 24 households, the Ashraf have a total population of 118 individuals, 60 male and 58 female, the

26. Malek-ul-Ulema Mufti Ismail Danishmand and his son Mufti Wali Danishmand successively held the post of chief Qazi. Their mazars at Village 'J' are the centre of pilgrimage for both Hindus and Muslims. The annual urs takes place on the 14th of Sha'ban, the eighth month of the lunar calender.

27. For Munshi Zakiuddin Ahmad's part in the struggle of 1857 see The Englishman, July 17, 1857, The Friend of India. July 23, 1857. pp. 698; also The Hindu Patriot, July 23, 1857.

28. Syed Ahmad Shaheed had vIsited Bhagalpur in 1242 A.D.

average family size being 4·91 and the male/female ratio being 1000 : 966. 41·66% of the families are of nuclear type, extended and complex types are 12.50% each and 29.16% are broken.

66.66% are landless, 8.33% have less than 1 bigha, 4.20% have 3 bighas, 4.30% have 5 bighas, 4.33% have 20 bighas, and 4.33% have 30 bighas of agricultural land.

4 (19.04%) of a total of 21 working hands are engaged in agricultural activities, 14.28% are in Government job, 23·80% are in private service, 9.52% are self-employed, 23.8% do petty business and 9.52% do casual work.

7.62% of the Ashraf are illiterate, 54·24% are educated and rest are just literate.

15. The Sheikh are one of the non-Ashraf community which functions as a beradari having a distinct social boundary of their own. This community of cultivators, agricultural labourers and dairy farmers has its population in both the villages of 'J' (Kundi) and 'P' (Dogachi). The population of this particular beradari of the Sheikh is confined to over half a dozen neighbouring villages within which their entire kinship network is confined.

The total number of households of the Sheikh in both the villages is 236, 86 in the Village 'J' (Kundi) and 150 in the Village 'P' (Dogachi), with 1095 individuals, 573 male and 522 female. The average size of the household is 4.64. 71.03% of the families are of nuclear type, 12.00% are extended, 2.12% are joint and complex types respectively, 4.23% are nascent, 2.55% are incomplete and 5.08% are broken.

In Village 'J' the percentage of landless in the community is 25·50. Seven individuals in Village 'J' own land ranging from 10 to 20 bighas and the rest own small plots for cultivation.

At Village 'J' out of a total of 113 working hands belonging to 86 households of the Sheikh 57 (50.44%) are day labourers, 6 (5.30%) are bidi rollers, 16 (14.15%) are cultivators, 2 (1.76%) are dairy farmers, 6 (5.30%) in Government jobs, 11 (9.73%) in private service, 8 (7.07%) in petty business and 1 (0.88%) is a technician.

At Village 'P' out of a total of 181 working hands belonging to 150 households 91 (50.27%) are daily wage earners, (10.55%) is bidi roller. 4 (2.20%) are masons, 19 (10.49%) are motor drivers, 5 (2.76%) are share croppers, 20 (11.40%) are cultivators, 7 (3.86%) are dairy farmers, 5 (2.96%) are serving Government and organised sector, 27 (14.91%) are in private service and 2 (1.10%) are in petty business.

69.90% of the Sheikh in Village 'J' (Kundi) are illiterate, 7.71% are educated and the rest are just literate.

55.77% of the members of the community in Village 'P' are illiterate and 14.46% are educated while the rest are just literate.

16. The Mansoori, having the traditional occupation of cotton carding are an endogamous group settled in Village 'P' in a separate hamlet known as Dogachi. Their settlements are mixed with the Sheikh. Mansoori maintain a separate boundary of their own through endogamy and a distinct mechanism of social control. The rules of marriage and patterns of kinship are, however, not very different from those of the Sheikh in their neighbourhood. Inter-relationship between the two is not hierarchical but based on equality in both the spheres of commensality and religious institutions. Unlike the Sheikh, the Mansoori are widespread not only in the state but beyond its boundaries and have their leadership at the state and national levels.

11 households of the Mansoori in the village consist of 62 individuals, 36 male and 26 female, the average size being 5.63 and male/female ratio is 1000 : 722. Family types among the Mansoori are 54.54% nuclear, 36.36% are extended and 9.09% are broken.

All the Mansoori housholds are landless. Of the 12 working hands in the 11 households 33.33% are daily wage earners, 8.33% are rickshaw pullers, 16.66% are in private service, 8.33% are motor mechanic and 25.00% in petty business.

56.00% are illiterates, 20.96% are educated and the rest are merely literate.

Having had some idea of the numerical strength of the relevant categories of people at the state and regional levels, having the potentiality of influencing the political developments in the area of study, we presented brief ethnographic notes on all the 16 castes and ethnic groups. This enables us to comprehend a very rough picture of their society, economy and level of development including land ownership, occupational patterns, educational attainment and ritual status of each of the groups.

We noted that out of the 13 Hindu Castes, one comes under the category of 'forward', 8 under the category of what is known as 'backward' (OBC) and 4 are scheduled castes. There are also three groups of Muslims, one belong to Ashraf category and 2 to the category of non-Ashraf. These groups of castes and communities, within a compact area of two adjacent villages, are fully representative of the categories required for the analysis of a pattern of inter-relationship relevant to our problem in a limlted area.

4

The Villages

Before going into the details of the castes and ethnic groups, bearing relevance to their inter-relationship, in the villages under observation, let us have some idea of the lay out of the villages, their settlement patterns and nature of dwelling houses in the same. For our convenience we shall call these villages as 'P' and 'J' respectively instead of mentioning their full name.

Situated on Bhagalpur-Baunsi Road within Jagdishpur Block, at a distance of about 7 and 9 kms. respectively southwards from Bhagalpur city, both the villages are adjacent to each other and are multi-ethnic. 'P' has 11 and 'J' has 10 ethnic groups or castes, 5 of whom are common to both the villages and 6 are exclusive to the former while 5 are exclusive to the latter.

The village 'P' is composed of one caste of the forward category, 6 belonging to backward castes and 3 to scheduled castes while 2 belonging to Muslim beradaries of non-Ashraf category. Similarly the village 'J' is composed of 6 backward castes, 2 scheduled castes and 2 to Muslim beradaries one belonging to Ashraf and another to non-Ashraf categories. Thus in both the villages there are altogether 16 castes or ethnic groups comprising 1 forward, 8 backward, 4 scheduled castes and 3 Muslim groups.

As it has been stated earlier the village 'P' had been under the former Zamindari of Kanaujia Brahmans, while village 'J' had been under the Zamindari of the Ashraf Sheikh, before the abolition of the system in 1962. The two villages are not of equal size. 'P' has an area of 243.26 hectares while 'J' consists of 77.29 hectares. 'P' has a population of 2592 while 'J' has a population of 1929 individuals. The Brahman constitute 17.73% of the total population of both villages, the backward 45.27%, the scheduled castes 8.78%, the Sheikh Ashraf 2.61% and non-Ashraf Muslims 25.59%

Both the villages have somewhat identical pattern in the sense that they are composed of several hamlets, often at considerable distance from each other. The hamlets are more like social units than the villages themselves. The hamlets have their specific names. The villages serve as revenue units but hamlets serve as social units, where specific ethnic groups or castes are settled, though not exclusively.

Settlement Pattern

It is interesting that the main settlement of both the villages 'P' and 'J' merge imperceptably with their neighbouring villages in different directions namely Baijani and Puraini respectively, while the hamlets belonging to the villages themselves are often at fair distance from them. Thus the boundaries of revenue village and village as a social unit do not coincide,

In village 'P' the Brahmans are settled in two different hamlets, the main or central part of the village and in Zamin, at a distance of over a furlong from the Central Zone. In the main village, the Brahman locality, though distinctly separated and having a wide area and commanding position, is not far from the settlements of the Dhanuk, the settlements of the Majrothi Jadav and the Tanti, which are hurdled together in the form of shapeless cluster. Some members of these castes work in the fields of their Brahman patrons either as seasonal day labour or as bonded labour and as domestic servants. In Zamin, a hamlet of village 'P' the Brahman locality is distinctly separate, but at a short distance, there is a cluster of settlements belonging to a few households of Tanti, Dhanuk and

Nai and in the outskirt of this hamlet there are a few households of the Dom, an untouchable caste who squat on the public land on the roadside at considerable distance from all the rest. A hamlet named Derhania is exclusively inhabited by the Sheikh while the Mansoori and the Sheikh have their settlements in yet another hamlet of village 'P' named Dogachi. This hamlet is flanked on one side by the settlements of the Barhai and on the other side by a cluster of Dosadh settlements. The Chamar settlement in village 'P' occurs over a furlong distance from the central part of the village occupied by the Brahmans. The settlement pattern of the village amply reflects the social distance where the settlements of the untouchable castes are more distant to the Brahman settlements than those of the clean Sudras.

In village 'J' the dominating sector of the main village is largely occupied by the Ashraf, the former Zamindars of their descendents in the village. They may be deemed as the counterpart of the Brahmans in village 'P'. The village 'J' consists of two hamlets, the main settlement and Kundi. In the main settlement the Ashraf live in close neighbourhood of the backward and untouchable castes namely the Nonia, the Jadav, the Tanti, the Gaurhi, the Barai, the Dhobi and Dosadh who are settled adjacent to the locality of the Ashraf, each having their distinct cluster of settlements. No distance is maintained by the Ashraf from the clusters of settlements of either the backward or the untouchables or scheduled castes. The distant hamlet of Kundi is also inhabited by the non-Ashraf Sheikh as well as the backward castes of Tanti and Nai. The clusters of the Muslim and non-Muslim settlements are distinct and separately segregated, but are in close neighbourhood and adjacent to each other.

Thus it is noticed that though differing in size, the two villages have identical pattern in being divided into a number of hamlets. There is also a common feature of having distinct clusters of settlements belonging to specific groups, castes or community within each of the hamlets. The hamlets are generally named and they function as social units, though interaction on the basis of caste or community, across hamlets is qualitatively more important

The Brahman settlements alone maintain greater physical distance in terms of space with the settlements of the untouchable castes. Their counterpart in Muslim society, the Ashraf, do not observe the distance with the untouchable castes either in terms of space or in certain matters of social interaction.

Both the villages have been electrified but while in village 'P' the electric poles do not go beyond the Brahman locality, and the streets passing through the localities inhabited by backward castes remain in darkness. The non-Brahman villagers attribute deliberateness in depriving them of this facility. In village 'J', however, the situation is different. The poles have been fixed deep into the exclusive areas of the backward castes and consumers of electricity include both backward and untouchable castes in fairly large numbers.

The dwelling houses in the villages in themselves do not show any distinctive pattern or significant difference on the basis of castes, except in case of Brahmans in village 'P' and Sheikh Ashraf in village 'J'. While a few brick-built structures are observed both in the localities of backward and scheduled castes, depending upon the pecuniary circumstances of their owners, most of the houses have mud walls and either thatched or tiled roofings on small plot of land. Palm leaves are also used for thatching.

The Brahman and Ashraf dwelling houses in their respective villages occupy larger areas and are generally brick-built, pucca structures with several rooms and both inner and outer courtyards.

The houses of the Ashraf, however, with the exception of one or two, give a picture of desolation and dilapidation, and are in a state of decay while the houses of the Brahmans are generally well maintained and in fairly good condition. A few houses have modern architectural designs.

Demographic Features

Though the demographic features relating to castes and communities in the villages may not appear to be directly related to the problem, they may illuminate certain aspects of inter-relationship and may enable us to make a comparative assessment of their incidence and their correlation with the background of the groups. The following tables present age groups and household size of the caste and communities in the two villages.

This small sample of the size of 833 households consisting of 3721 individuals, belonging to 16 castes and enthic groups inhabiting the two contiguous villages may not enable us to make valid generalisations, yet certain definite trends may be discerned from the data at our disposal (Tables 9 and 10).

The data indicates that the frequency distribution of age groups 0-5 years is identical among the Brahmnns (10.37) and Sheikh Ashraf (10.16). This may indicate that the procreative habits of the Brahman and Ashraf do not differ in any significant measure. They, however, differ sharply with the backward and scheduled castes as also the non-Ashraf Muslim beradaries who with the exception of a few groups like the Dom and the Mansoori, provide evidence of identical procreative habits. Both Brahmans and Ashraf have realised the need for limiting births only in recent years.

In the matter of family size, the Ashraf and Brahman sharply differ. The average size of the Ashraf household was found to be 4.11 while that of the Brahman was 8.10. Brahman households on an average was largest of all the groups in our sample. Being a major land owning community in the rural setting this may not be unnatural and as we shall see in subsequent tables the frequency of extended and joint type of families among them is significant.

The Brahmans and the Ashraf also differ sharply in Male-Female ratio in their groups. Among the Brahmans there are 782 female per 1000 male, while the Ashraf have 966 female per 1000 male.

The causes of the unusually smaller proportion of female among the Brahman need thorough probing. It will not be appropriate to jump into conclusions, but usually this phenomenon characterise a society where the status of women is low and female child is not given the quality of treatment allowed to the male and also the evils of dowry is present in acute form.

The sex ratio among the Chamar (1000 : 1000) and the Dhanuk (1000 : 1004) is excellently balanced. Maximum disbalance is found among the Dom (1000 : 529) and the Barhai (1000 : 666) but it is based on a very small sample. Muslim groups of Sheikh (1000 : 910) based on the average of the two villages, and Ashraf (1000 : 966) present a fairy balanced sex ratio but Mansoori (1000 : 966) present a fairly balanced sex ratio but Monsoori (1000 : 722) do not conform to the pattern.

The samples are small enough to enable us to make sweeping generalisation but these are comparatively larger point to certain symptoms and probably it will not be absolutely incorrect to correlate it with certain values in the society. The adverse ratio of the female would indicate the position of women and the degree of neglect to the female child. The hue and cry that is raised at the national level only helps impairing relationship on issues that may be non-existent or do not have substantiated sociological basis.

Family Types

Some idea of the family types among the caste ond ethnic groups in the two villages may be had from the following tables. Nascent families are those that are composed of only husband and wife who have'nt had offsprings as yet and incomplete families are composed of such couples who do not live with their offsprings or did not have children and do not except children any more. Extended families are those which are composed of a spouse, their male son or sons with their wife or wives, and joint families comprise two or more brothers living together with their spouse.

Despite a rural setting where the society in tradition bound the nuclear type of family predominates. Among all the castes and communities, this type of family is largest in proportion to other types. There may be a variety of factors contributing to the process of nucleation, but the most important one is the independent source of income. Landlessness has a definite correlation with higher incidence of nuclear

TABLE 9

Showing Age-Groups and House hold Size of Caste and Communities in Village 'P'

Sl. No.	*Group*	*No. of House-hold*	*Population*	*Male*	*Female*	*Age*	
						0-5 Yrs.	*6-10 Yrs.*
1.	Brahmans	99	802	450	352	88 10.37	121 15.08
2.	Jadav	18	91	51	40	16 17.58	17 18.68
3.	Dhanuk	35	175	86	89	35 20.00	31 17.71
4.	Nai	13	76	41	35	12 15.78	19 25.00
5.	Tanti	65	360	194	166	80 22.22	69 19.16
6.	Barhi	9	55	33	22	7 12.72	14 25.45

7.	Dosadh (Paswan)	24	98	55	43	18 18.36	19 19.36
8.	Chamar	30	128	64	64	29 22.65	21 16.40
9.	Dom	6	26	17	9	2 7.69	6 23.07
10.	Mansoori	11	62	36	26	8 12.90	13 20.96
11.	Sheikh	150	719	376	343	162 22.53	109 15.15
12.	All Groups	460	2592	1403	1189	457 17.63	439 16.93

(*Cont.*)

Sl. No.	Group	Groups					Average Family Size
		11-20 Yrs.	21-30 Yrs.	31-40 Yrs.	41-50 Yrs	51 & Above	
1.	Brahmans	185 23.06	151 18.82	94 11.72	73 9.10	90 11.22	8.10
2.	Jadav	17 18.68	13 14.28	8 8.79	12 13.18	8 8.79	5.05
3.	Dhanuk	26 14.85	31 17.71	29 16.57	14 8.00	9 5.14	5.00
4.	Nai	14 18.42	11 14.47	11 14.47	5 6.57	4 5.26	5.84
5.	Tanti	43 11.34	63 17.50	43 11.34	38 10.55	24 6.66	5.53
6.	Barhai	15 27.27	4 7.27	5 9.09	5 9.09	5 9.09	6.11
7.	Dosadh (Paswan)	11 11.22	16 16.32	10 10.20	16 16.32	8 8.16	4.08

		14	28	11	8	17	
8.	Chamar	10.93	21.87	8.59	6.26	13.28	4.16
		7	2	6	2	1	
9.	Dom	26.32	7.69	23.07	7.69	3.84	4.33
		15	10	4	4	8	
10.	Mansoori	24.19	16.12	6.45	6.45	12.90	5.63
		119	134	89	57	49	
11.	Seikh	16.55	18.63	12.37	7.32	6.81	4.74
		466	463	310	234	223	
12.	All Groups	17.97	17.86	11.95	9.02	8.60	5.63

TABLE 10

Showing Age-Group and House hold Size of Castes and Communities in Village 'J'

Sl. No.	*Group*	*No. of House-hold*	*Population*	*Male*	*Female*	*Age*	
						0-5 Yrs.	*6-10 Yrs.*
1.	Sheikh Ashraf	24	118	60	58	12 10.16	17 14.40
2.	Sheikh	86	373	197	179	82 21.80	51 13.57
3.	Jadav	60	383	193	190	72 18.79	63 16.44
4.	Tanti	122	580	310	270	122 21.03	79 13.62
5.	Gourhi	17	98	50	48	24 24.48	17 17.34

6. Nonia	27	178	96	82	39 21.91	28 15.73
7. Barai	2	14	8	6	5 35.71	2 14.28
8. Nai	7	37	21	16	6 16.21	8 21.62
9. Dosadh (Paswan)	19	95	54	41	19 20.00	12 12.63
10. Dhobi	9	50	29	21	12 24.00	8 16.00
11. All Groups	373	1929	1018	911	393 20.37	285 14.77

(Cont.)

Sl. No.	Group	Groups					Average Family Size
		11-20 Yrs.	21-30 Yrs.	31-40 Yrs.	41-50 Yrs.	51 & Above	
1.	Sheikh Ashraf	24 21.42	23 20.53	14 11.86	10 8.47	18 15.25	4.11
2.	Sheikh	71 18.88	57 15.15	44 11.70	35 9.30	36 9.57	4.37
3.	Jadav	69 18.01	69 18.01	47 12.27	28 7.31	35 9.13	6.38
4.	Tanti	110 18.67	109 18.96	76 13.10	37 6.37	47 8.10	4.15
5.	Gourhi	12 12.24	14 14.28	13 13.26	12 12.24	6 6.12	5.76
6.	Nonia	32 17.97	30 16.85	17 9,55	19 16.67	13 7.30	6.59

7. Barahi	1 7.14		4 28.56		2 14.28	7.00
8. Nai	7 18.91	4 10.81	6 16.21	4 10.81	2 5.40	5.28
9. Dosadh (Paswan)	12 12.63	21 22.10	10 10.52	10 10.52	11 11.57	5.00
10. Dhobi	9 18.00	4 8.00	5 10.00	5 10.00	7 14.00	5.55
11. All Groups	347 17.98	331 17.59	236 12.23	160 8.29	177 9.17	5.12

TABLE 11

Showing Family Types of Castes/Ethnic Groups in Village 'P'

Sl. No. Group	Type of Family							Total Number of Huose-Holds
	Nuclear	*Nascent*	*Incom-plete*	*Extended*	*Joint*	*Complex*	*Broken*	
1. Brahman	40 40.40	3 2.02		38 38.38	12 12.12	2 2.02	5 5.05	99
2. Jadav	14 77.00			4 22.22				18
3. Dhanuk	20 57.14	2 5.71		6 17.14	3 8.57		4 11.42	35
4. Nai	8 61.53	2 15.38		2 15.38	1 7.69			13
5. Tanti	33 50.76		5 7.69	20 30.76	1 1.53	2 3.07	4 6.15	65
6. Barhi	5 55.00		2 22.00	2 22.00				9

7. Dosadh (Paswan)	13 54.16	1 4.16	2 8.33	3 12.50			5 20.83	6
8. Chamar	21 70.00		3 10.00	4 13.33			2 6.66	30
9. Dom	4 66.66	1 67.66		1 16.66				6
10. Mansoori	6 54.54			4 36.36			11 9.09	21
11. Sheikh	111 74.00	6 4.00	3 2.00	22 14.66	3 2.00		5 3.33	150
12. All Groups	275 59.78	14 3.04	15 3.26	106 23.04	20 4.34	4 0.86	5 5.65	470

TABLE 12

Showing Family Types of Caste/Ethnic Groups in Village 'J'

Sl. No.	*Groups*	*Type of Family*							*Total No. of House-Holds*
		Nuclear	*Nascent*	*Incomplete*	*Extended*	*Joint*	*Complex*	*Broken*	
1.	Sheikh Ashraf	10 41.66			3 12.50	1 4.16	3 12.50	7 29.16	24
2.	Sheikh	59 68.60	4 4.65	3 3.48	6 6.37	2 2.32	5 5.81	7 8.13	86
3.	Jadav	30 50.00	2 3.33	1 1.66	15 25.00	2 3.33	8 13.33	2 3.33	60
4.	Tanti	70 57.37	4 3.27	7 5.73	30 24.59	2 1.63	4 3.27	5 4.09	122
5.	Gourhi	4 23.52		1 5.88	9 52.34			3 17.64	17
6.	Nonia	15 55.50	1 3.70	1 3.70	8 29.62		2 7.40		27

7. Barai	2 100.00							2
8. Nai	4 57.14			1 14.28	1 14.28		1 14.28	7
9. Dosadh (Paswan)	5 26.31	1 5.56	1 5.26	8 42.10		2 10.52	2 10.52	19
10. Dhobi	4 44.44	1 11.11		3 33.33	1 11.11			9
11. All Groups	203 54.42	13 3.75	14 3.75	83 22.25	9 2.41	24 6.43	27 7.23	373

family, though it may not be the only cause for nucleation. We find that some caste of Jadav show variation in the incidence of nuclear families in the two different villages. In village 'P' where they are totally landless it is 77.00% while in village 'J' where 70.00% of them own agricultural land the percentage of nuclear family is 59.00%.

It is significant that the incidence of nuclear families is almost indentical among the Brahman (40.40%) and the Ashraf Sheikh (41.66%). Among the backward and scheduled castes it varies from 55.50 to 100.00% with the exception of the Gourhi (23.52%) and the Dhoei (44.44%) which can be explained on the basis of the nature of their occupations involving larger number of people in their functioning.

Next in importance is the incidence of extended family type and it is highest among the Brahman (38.38%) and none at all among the Barai. The percentage of broken families is higest among the Sheikh Ashraf (29.16%) and none among the Nonia, Barai, Dhobi, Barahai and the Dom.

Land Ownership

The pattern of land ownership by different castes indicate the real difference. Over 85% of the Brahman household own agricultural land from 3 to over 50 bighas, only two households are in the category of 50 and above and the largest holding does not exceed 90 bighas. 25.00% of the Sheikh Ashraf own 3 to 30 bighas. Only one household owns 30 bighas.

Tables 13 and 14 provide the details of the amount of land owned by each caste and ethnic group in villages 'P' and 'J' respectively. In village 'P' 4(3.76%); 10(15.38%) and 9(33.34%) the households belonging to Nai, Tanti and Barai castes respectively own agricultural land ranging from 1 to 3 bighas and 1(3.33% household of the Chamar own 7 bighas of agricultural land. All the other backward and Scheduled castes are landless. Among the two Muslim beradaries in the village the Mansoori are totally landless but

24.66% of the non-Ashraf Shehikh own land from 1 to 15 bighas. Only one individual owns 15 bighas.

In village 'J' the pattern of land ownership is quite different. Here not only the backward and scheduled castes, with the exception of Barai, owns agricultural land but some of the backward castes namely Jadav and Nonia have far superseded the Ashraf, the former Zamindars of the village, in matter of land ownership. Here 65.00% of the Jadav households own land from 1 to 45 bighas, 37.00% of the Nonia own land from 2 to 10 bighas while only 29.66% of the Ashraf own land from 1 to 30 bighas. Only two households of the Ashraf own 20 and 30 bighas respectively and the rest of the land owing households of the Ashraf come in the category of 1 to 3 bighas. 45.34% of the non-Ashraf Sheikh own from 1 to 20 bighas. This indicates a large scale land alienation from the Ashraf to other castes or ethnic groups. A comparative picture of the pattern of land ownership by the scheduled and backward castes in both the villages 'P' and 'J' may be had from the following Tables 15 and 16 respectively.

Occupational Pursuits

The occupational pursuits significantly followed by individuals belonging to various castes and communities, having been grouped into 17 categories, it was noticed in village 'P' (see table 17) that unskilled daily wage earners mainly belonging to Tanti, Dhanuk, Jadav and Dosadh castes as also the Muslim beradaries of non-Ashraf Sheikh and the Mansoori. The Nai, the Chamar and the Dom, figure insignificantly in the group of daily wage earners. A spurt in the construction industry in the nearby city of Bhagalpur has provided an opportunity for these people to work for loading and unloading of sand lorries and also to work as aids to masons in the construction work. Despite this work for these people is available on an average for three to four days in a week, full employment is available only during the agricultural season which does not last more than a couple of months in a year.

TABLE 13

Agricultural Land Ownership by Groups in Village 'P'

Sl. No. Group	*No Land*	*Up to 5 Kathas*	*Up to 10 Kathas*	*Up to 1 Bighas*	*Up to 3 Bighas*	*Up to 5 Bighas*	*Up to 7 Bighas*	*Up to 10 Bighas*	*Up to 15 Bighas*
1	2	3	4	5	6	7	8	9	10
1. Brahman	11	1	1	21	19	9	11	13	5
2. Jadav	18	—	—	—	—	—	—	—	—
3. Dhanuk	35	—	—	—	—	—	—	—	—
4. Nai	9	—	—	1	5	—	—	—	—
5. Tanti	55	—	4	2	4	—	—	—	—
6. Barhai	6	—	—	2	1	—	—	—	—
7. Dosadh (Paswan)	24	—	—	—	—	—	—	—	—

8. Chamar	29	—	—	—	—	—	1	—	—
9. Dom	6	—	—	—	—	—	—	—	—
10. Mansoori	11	—	—	—	—	—	—	—	—
11. Sheikh	98	11	4	10	15	2	7	2	1

(Cont.)

TABLE 13 (*Cont.*)

Sl. No. Group	*Upto 20 Bighas*	*Upto 25 Bighas*	*Upto 30 Bighas*	*Upto 35 Bighas*	*Upto 40 Bighas*	*Upto 45 Bighas*	*Upto 50 Bighas*	*Above 50 Bighas*	*Total No. of House-hold*
11	12	13	14	15	16	17	18	19	20
1. Brahman	—	2	1	2	—	—	—	2	99
2. Jadav	—	—	—	—	—	—	—	—	18
3. Dhanuk	—	—	—	—	—	—	—	—	35
4. Nai	—	—	—	—	—	—	—	—	13
5. Tanti	—	—	—	—	—	—	—	—	65
6. Barhai	—	—	—	—	—	—	—	—	9
7. Dosadh (Paswan)	—	—	—	—	—	—	—	—	24

8. Chamar	—	—	—	—	—	—	—	—	30
9. Dom	—	—	—	—	—	—	—	—	6
10. Mansoori	—	—	—	—	—	—	—	—	11
11. Sheikh	—	—	—	—	—	—	—	—	150

* 1 Acre=2 Bigha.s ** $2\frac{1}{2}$ Dec.=1 Katha.

TABLE 14

Agricultural Land Ownership by Groups in Village 'J'

S. No. Group	*No Land*	*Upto 5 Kathas*	*Upto 10 Kathas*	*Upto 1 Bighas*	*Upto 3 Bighas*	*Upto 5 Bighas*	*Upto 7 Bighas*	*Upto 10 Bighas*	*Upto 15 Bighas*
1	2	3	4	5	6	7	8	9	10
1. Sheikh Ashraf	16	—	1	1	1	3	—	—	—
2. Sheikh	22	17	8	5	22	4	1	6	—
3. Jadav	9	9	3	6	13	7	7	2	2
4. Tanti	37	45	7	22	9	1	—	—	—
5. Gourhi	—	13	1	5	—	—	—	—	—
6. Nonia	10	7	—	2	2	2	3	1	—
7. Barai	2	—	—	—	—	—	—	—	—
8. Nai	—	4	1	2	—	—	—	—	—
9. Dosadh (Paswan)	14	4	—	1	—	—	—	—	—
10. Dhobi	5	—	—	1	2	1	—	—	—

TABLE 14 (*Cont.*)

Sl. No.	*Group*	*Upto 20 Bighas*	*Upto 25 Bighas*	*Upto 30 Bighas*	*Upto 35 Bighas*	*Upto 40 Bighas*	*Upto 45 Bighas*	*Upto 50 Bighas*	*Abovo 50 Bighas*	*Total No. of House-hold*
	11	12	13	14	15	16	17	18	19	20
1.	Sheikh Ashraf	1	—	1	—	—	—	—	—	24
2.	Sheikh	1	—	—	—	—	—	—	—	86
3.	Jadav	—	1	—	—	—	1	—	—	60
4.	Tanti	1	—	—	—	—	—	—	—	122
5.	Gourhi	—	—	—	—	—	—	—	—	17
6.	Nonia	—	—	—	—	—	—	—	—	27
7.	Barai	—	—	—	—	—	—	—	—	2
8.	Nai	—	—	—	—	—	—	—	—	7
9.	Dosadh (Paswan)	—	—	—	—	—	—	—	—	19
10.	Dhobi	—	—	—	—	—	—	—	—	9

*1 Acre=2 Bighas. ** $2\frac{1}{2}$ Dec.=1 Katha.

TABLE 15

Comparative Picture of Land Ownership by Scheduled Castes in both Village 'P' and 'J'

Sl. No.	*Castes*		*No. of House-hold*	*Popula-lation*	*Male*	*Female*	*Land Ownership*				
							Landless	*Upto 5 Katha*	*Upto 1 Bighas*	*Upto 3 Bighas*	*Upto 7 Bighas*
1.	Paswan (Dosadh)	**P**	24	98	55	43	24 100.00				
		J	19	95	54	41	14 73.68	4 21.05	1 5.26		

	P	6	26	17	9	6			
						100.00			
2. Dom									
	J								
	P	30	128	64	64	29			1
						96.66			3.33
3. Chamar									
	J								
	P								
4. Dhobi									
	J	9	50	29	21	5	1	2	1
						55.55	11.11	22.22	11.11

TABLE 16

Comparative Picture of Land Ownership by Backward Castes in Village 'P' and 'J'

Sl. No.	*Group*		*No. of House-hold*	*Popula-tion*	*Male*	*Female*	*Land-less*	*Land Ownership* Upto 5 Kathas	*Upto 1 Bigha*	*Upto 3 Bighas*	*Upto 7 Bighas*	*Upto 10 Bighas*	*Upto 15 Bighas*	*Upto 20 Bighas*	*Upto 45 Bighas*
							55		6	4					
1.	Tanti	P	65	360	194	166	84.61		9.23	6.51					
							37	45	29	9	1			1	
		J	122	580	310	270	30.23	36.88	23.77	7.37	0.81			0.81	
							35								
2.	Dhanuk	P	35	175	86	89	100.00								
		J													
		P													
								13	4						
3.	Gaurhi	J	17	98	50	48		76.47	23.52						

4. Barai	P											
	J	2	14	8	6	2 100.00						
5. Nonia	P											
	J	27	178	96	82	10 37.03 18	7 25.92	2 7.40	2 7.40	5 18.51	1 3.70	
6. Jadav	P	18	91	51	40	100.00						
	J	60	383	193	190	9 13.00 9	9 15.00	9 15.00 1	13 21.66 3	14 23 33	2 3.33	2 3.33
7. Nai	P	13	76	41	35	69.23						
	J	7	37	21	16	6	4 57.14	3 42.05 2	1			
8. Barhai	P	9	55	33	22	66.66		22.22	11.11			
	J											

The age old tradition of bonded labour has not ceased to persist in village 'P' where at least 11 individuals belong to Jadav, Dhanuk, Tanti and Chamar castes continue to serve the landowners as bonded labour.

It was also noticed that the benefit of the fixation of minimum wages by the Government agencies is quite often denied to the daily wage earners when they are employed by village land owners ond influential people. Owing to a very high percentage of landlessness the supply of daily wage earners is much more than their demand, large scale seasonal migrations take place to neighbouring states of West Bengal and Assam and to distant areas of Punjab and western Uttar Pradesh.

The village being closer to the city, the toiling castes are more fortunate here than in comparatively distant or remote villages because it provides them opportunity for employment and to a considerably more enterprising among them to engage themselves in such jobs as rickshaw pulling. The Chamars have entered into the occupation in a significant number followed by the Nai, the Dhanuk, the Tanti and the Mansoori. Bidi rolling is less popular in village 'P' than in 'J', and here it is mainly pursued by the Tanti.

Traditional occupation no longer remain a source of sustenance to the people. It is significant only in case of the Barhai, all of whom are engaged in carpentery work and the Dom who are employed as scavengers. Only a very insignificantly small number of Brahman, the Chamar and the Jadav are engaged in their respective traditional occupations of priesthood, shoe-making and dairy work. The vast bulk of the members of these castes as also the Nai, the Tanti and the Mansoori have nothing to do with their respective traditional occupations.

The sectors of the village inhabited by the backward and scheduled castes as well as the Sheikh and the Mansoori, with rare exceptions, give a picture of overcrowding and proverty. Judged from the living standards of these people, the masons, the carpenters, the motor drivers and those few of them who are employed as lower grade employees of the Government are envied for their comparatively better standard of life on account of the higher daily wages or monthly salaries they draw. But only a fortunate few are in this category.

Share cropping is done by the Jadav, the Nai, the Tanti, the Chamar and the Sheikh on land mainly belonging to the Brahmans but cultivation on own land is done by the Brahman and the Sheikh, the former are medium and big cultivators while the Sheikh are small cultivators.

By far the largest number of service holders under the Government, the organised sector, and private industrial and commercial concerns are Brahmans. They alone are employed in the scheduled banks, particularly the State Bank of India where they hold complete monopoly over the jobs, with the exception of all others. The jobs they hold include responsible posts in the Army and Air Force, in Public Works Department, Military Engineering Service, in various capacities in the District Court, in the State Transport Department, in Irrigation Department, as teachers etc. etc. A few members of the backward and Scheduled castes have also found their way into the State or private service but they are mainly employed as peons and sweepers or safaiwalas or as lower grade employees.

Physicians and vaids as well as contractors of sand lorries also belong exclusively to the Brahman caste. The Bramans in village 'P' enjoy a dominant position not only in matter of land ownership but also in nature of occupational pursuits, holding a virtual monopoly of profitable jobs. This dominance is complete so far the backward and the scheduled castes are concerned. Their position vis-a-vis the Sheikh is somewhat different. No one from the Sheikh serves them as bonded labour, though the Sheikh are no better than the Backward castes. Their relative freedom from dominance of the affluent Brahmans has resulted in their entry into the occupations of motor driving, masonary work, dairy farming, beside ciltivation on whatever land they possess. A number of them come to Calcutta and occasionally go to Delhi and elsewhere to work in private industrial and commercial establishments.

The occupational pattern of village 'J' (see Table 18), an erstwhile Zamindari of the Ashraf, is somewhat different. Here

TABLE 17

Primary Occupation of Castes and Ethnic Groups in Village 'P'

Sl. No.	*Groups*	*No. of House-hold*	*Total Population*	*Day Labourer*	*Rickahaw Puller*	*Bidi Roller*	*Mason*	*Motor Driver*	*Share Cropper*	*Cultivator*	*Dairy Worker*
1.	Brahman	99	802					6 3.61		18 10.84	
2.	Jadav	18	91	11 47.82			2 8.69		1 4.34		2 8.69
3.	Dhanuk	35	175	23 54.76	3 7.14		1 2.38				
4.	Nai	13	76	2 15.38	2 15.38				2 15.38	1 7.69	
5.	Tanti	65	360	50 58.82	1 1.17	8 9.41	3 3.52	2 2.35	4 4.70		
6.	Barhai	9	55								
7.	Dosadh	24	98	18 72.00							

8. Chamar	30	128	5 15.62	18 56.25				2 6.25		
9. Dom	6	26	1 14.28							
10. Mansoori	11	62	4 33.33	1 8.33			1 8.33			
11. Sheikh	150	719	91 50.27		1 0.55	4 2.20	19 10.49	5 2.76	20 11.04	7 3.81
12. All Groups	460	2592	205 34.45	25 4.20	9 1.51	10 1.68	28 4,70	14 2.35	39 6.55	9 1.51

(*Cont.*)

TABLE 17 (*Cont.*)

Sl. No.	*Groups*	*Govt. is Service & Org. Sec.*	*Servlce Bank*	*Service Private*	*Technical Work*	*Petty Business*	*Traditio-nal Occu-pation*	*Casual Work*	*Iudepen-dent Prof.*	*Bonded Labour*	*Total No. of Worker*
1.	Brahman	56	37	19	2	19	3		6		166
		33.73	22.28	11.14	1.20	11.44	1.80		3.66		
2.	Jadav			2				2		3	23
				8.69				8.69		13.04	
3.	Dhanuk	2		11		1				1	42
		4.76		26.19		2.38				2.38	
4.	Nai	5			1						13
		38.46			7.59						
5.	Tanti	3		4		3		2		5	85
		3.52		4.70		3.52		2.35		5.88	
6.	Barhai						9				9
							100.00				
7.	Dosadh	3		3	1						25
		12.00		12.00	4.00						

8. Chamar	1		2			1	1		2	35
	3.12		6.25			3.12	3.12		6.25	
9. Dom	6									7
	85.71									
10. Mansoori			2	1	3					12
			16.66	8.33	25.00					
11. Sheikh	5		27		2					181
	2.76		14.94		1.10					
12. All Groups	81	37	70	5	28	13	5	6	11	595
	13.61	6.21	17.76	0.67	4.70	2.35	0.84	1.00	1.84	

TABLE 18

Primary Occupations of Castes and Ethnic Groups in Village 'J'

Sl. No.	*Group*	*No. of Household*	*Total Popu- lation*	*Day Labourer*	*Rickshaw Puller*	*Bidi Roller*	*Mason*	*Motor Driver*	*Share Cropper*	*Cultiva- tor*	*Daily Worker*
1.	Sheikh Ashraf	24	118							4 19.04	
2.	Sheikh	86	376	57 53.27		6 5.60				16 14.95	2 1.86
3.	Jadav	60	383	12 13.95		8 9.30		3 3.40		22 25.58	13 15.11
4.	Tanti	122	580	46 26.43		85 48.85	3 1.72	4 2.29		12 6.89	1
5.	Gourhi	17	98	2 5.71	1 2.85						
6.	Nonia	27	178	3 8.33	1 2.77	18 50.00		1 2.77		3 8.33	
7.	Barhai	2	14								

8. Nai	7	37	2							
			22.22							
9. Dosadh	19	95	5	1	14	1				
			16.66	3.33	46.66	3.33				
10. Dhobi	9	50	1						2	
			9.09						18.18	
11. All Groups	373	1929	188	2	131	4	8		59	16
			25.04	0.58	25.63	0.78	1.56		11.54	3.13

(*Cont.*)

TABLE 18 (*Cont.*)

Sl. No.	*Group*	*Service Govt. & Org. Sec.*	*Service Bank*	*Service Private*	*Technical Worker*	*Petty Business*	*Traditional Occupation*	*Casual Worker*	*Independent Prof.*	*Bonded Labour*	*Total No. of Workers*
1.	Sheikh	3		5	2	5		2			21
	Ashraf	14.28		23.80	9.52	23.80		9.52			
2.	Sheikh	6		11	1	8					107
		5.60		10.28	0.93	7.47					
3.	Jadav	17	1	5	5	5					86
		19.76	1.16	5.81		5.81					
4.	Tanti			4	3	12		4			174
				2.29	1.72	6.89		2.29			
5.	Gourhi			6		26					35
				17.14		74.28					
6.	Nonia	1		2		7					36
		2.77		5.55		19.44					
7.	Barhai					2					2
						100.00					

8. Nai						7 77.77		9
9. Dosadh	5 16.66		1 3.33		3 10.00			30
10. Dhobi	4 36.36					4 36.36		11
11. All Groups	36 7.04	1	34 6.65	6 1.17	68 13.30	11 2.15	6 1.17	511

the percentage of the unskilled landless labourer is comparatively smaller than the village 'P'. The pattern of land ownership due mainly to land transfers from the Sheikh Ashraf to the Backward and Scheduled Castes of Jadav, Nonia and Dhobi, is partly responsible for this situation. Some members of the Backward and Scheduled Castes continue to be engaged in such marginal occupations as bidi rolling, an important occupation in the village mainly pursued by the Tanti, Nonia and the Dosadh. One individual each belonging to Nonia, Gourhi and Dosadh castes has taken to rickshaw driving which they own. The Jadav and the Dhobi have entered into Government and organised sector jobs in which their percentage is much higher than those of the Ashraf Sheikh. A solitary bank employee working as a guard hails from the Jadav caste. The Jadav are not only in lower grade jobs but hold posts of police officers and military men, besides being college lecturers.

Though neither the numerical strength of the Ashraf nor their economic condition or political importance today, justifies any amount of their capability to exercise dominance over others in the village, their behaviour in the past, during their hay-day of Zamindari and land ownership, with rare exceptions, was not repressive to the Backward and Scheduled castes. They did exercise their power and prerogative as Zamindars and land owners, but the attitude of keeping the backward perpetually in the state of backwardness did not occur to them as it is observed in village 'P'. The result was that instead of standing in the way of the backwards they offered help to some of the members of these castes, as it is narrated by a retired police officer belonging to Jadav community. They did their best in helping a few individuals belonging to Jadav and Nonia castes in the village in their education and employment. This paved the way to a considerable transformation in the respective communities.

Educational Status

For an impoverished, landless and backward section of society, mainly concentrating in less lucrative marginal occupations for its sustenance, the only non-violent way for socio-economic uplift was appropriate education, not only for due participation in the structure of opportunities but also for adequate consciousness to resist exploitation. But it appears that the Backward and Scheduled Castes as well as non-Ashraf Muslim communities are far from benefitting from education.

Leaving aside a few very small groups of Barhai and Dom, the percentage of illiteracy ranges from 56 to 77. Even if we take a very liberal definition of literate as those who can read and can sign their name, and educated as those who have read up to class III or are reading in the class, we get a very dismal picture of the percentage of educated among the Backward and Scheduled castes as well as the non-Ashraf Muslim ethnic groups (see Tables 19 and 20) in both the villages 'P' and 'J'. With this extremely liberal definition of 'educated' we find that barring a few small groups of Barhai, Nai, Mansoori and Dom in village 'P' the percentage of educated varies between 5.49 and 14.46. The percentage of illiteracy among the Brahman is 3.36 in which mostly old women are found to occur who were denied education some 50 to 60 years ago. The percentage of educated among the Brahmans is 71.07.

The position in village 'J' is considerably different where the Jadav, the Nonia and the Dhobi have made considerable headway, though the Sheikh Ashraf maintain their lead in percentage of educated (54.23).

Having sub-divided the educated into two distinct categories of (1) those who complete their education and (2) those who are still receiving education among all the castes and communities in the two villages we get a clear picture of the state of education in comparative terms. Lookiug at the first category comprising those who have completed their education and are no longer in the process of formally receiving the same in village 'P' we note that 32.75 per cent of the Brahmans come within this category while the percentage of Jadav (1.09), Dhanuk (4.00). Nai (4.44), Tanti (3.88), Barhai (2.00), Dosadh (3.05). Chamar (1.56), Dom (3.85), Mansoori (2.22) and Sheikh (3.61) are insignificant.

TABLE 19

Literacy and Educational Status of Castes and Communities in Village 'P'

Sl. No.	*Group*	*No. of House-holds*	*No. of Indi-viduals*	*Illiterate*	*Literate*	*Education Achieved*	*Education Receiving*	*Total Educated*
1.	Brahman	99	802	27	116	269	301	570
				3.36		33.54	37.53	71.07
2.	Jadav	18	91	69	1	1	4	5
				75.82		1.09	4.39	5.49
3.	Dhanuk	35	175	103	9	7	12	19
				58.85		4.00	6.85	10.85
4.	Nai	13	76	42	1	11	9	20
				55.26		14,47	11.84	26.31
5.	Tanti	15	360	227	10	14	26	40
				76.94		3.88	7.22	11.11
6.	Barhai	9	55	22	2	11	15	26
				40.00		20.00	27.27	47.27
7.	Dosadh	24	98	69	3	3	6	9
				70.40		3.06	6.12	9.18

8. Chamar	30	128	86 67.18		2 1.56	9 7.03	11 8.59
9. Dom	6	26	8 30.76	7	1 3.84	8 30.76	9 34.61
10. Mansoori	11	62	35 56.00	8	2 3.22	11 17.74	13 20.96
11. Sheikh	150	719	401 55.77	35	30 4.17	74 10.29	104 14.46
12. All Groups	460	2592	1089	192	351	475	826

TABLE 20

Literacy and Educational Status of Castes and Communities In Village 'J'

Sl. No.	*Groups*	*No. of House-hoids*	*No. of Indi-viduals*	*Illiterate*	*Literate*	*Education Achieved*	*Education Receiving*	*Total Educated*
1.	Sheikh Ashraf	24	118	9	32	31	33	64
				7.62		26.27	27.96	54.23
2.	Sheikh	86	376	229	27	15	14	29
				69.90		3.98	3.72	7.71
3.	Jadav	60	383	191	30	41	52	93
				49.86		10.70	13.57	24.28
4.	Tanti	122	580	341	51	20	48	68
				58.79		3.44	8.27	11.72
5.	Gourhi	17	98	49	25	11	13	24
				50.00		11.22	13.26	24.48
6.	Nonia	27	178	64	26	16	29	45
				35.95		8.98	16.29	25.28
7.	Barai	2	14	3		3	4	7
				21.42		21.42	28.57	50.00

8. Nai	7	37	28 75.67		1 2.10	2 5.40	3 8.10
9. Dosadh	19	95	66 69.47		6 6.31	4 4.21	10 10.52
10. Dhobi	9	50	14 28.00	4	8 16.00	16 32.00	24 45.00
11. All Groups	373	1929	934	145	152	165	367

But even these figures do not give the correct picture of the educational status of the castes and communities in the village. If we take into account the level of education achieved by the respective communities, the position will be clear. Of the 9 individuals in village 'P' who have technical or professional qualifications only one belongs to Tanti caste who has received training in weaving silk and all the other 8 are Brahmans who have obtained degree in Mechanical Engineering (3), R.M.P. (1), B.Ed. (2) and Law (2). All the 12 post graduates and 50 graduates are Brahmans while out of 37 undergraduates also belong to Brahman caste. Similarly 54 out of 75 matriculates and 50 out of 74 individuals who have read only up to class X are Brahmans. The insignificance of the Backward and the Scheduled Castes as well as Muslim ethnic groups is clear (Table 21).

The position in village 'J', where the previous generation of the Ashraf, the erstwhile Zamindars had taken considerable interest in the educational endeavours of the Backward castes is somewhat different. Here out of 3 post graduates two belong to the Jadav caste and one to the Ashraf. Similarly out of 13 graduates 5 belong to Sheikh Ashraf, 5 to non-Ashraf Sheikh and one each to Jadav, Tanti and Gourhi caste, and out of 12 individuals who have read up to under-graduate level 4 belong to Ashraf Sheikh, 5 to non-Ashraf Sheikh, 2 to Jadav and one to Nai castes. Of the 29 matriculates 8 belong to Ashraf, 4 to non-Ashraf Sheikh, 4 to Jadav, 1 to Tanti, 6 to Nonia, 3 to Dosadh and 3 to Dhobi castes. In the category of those who have read up to class X the Backward castes predominate. It is interesting that while the previous generation of the Ashraf was instrumental in popularising education in the village among the Backward castes, the present generation of their own community has receded backward and appears to be downwardly mobile (Table-22).

Looking at the category of those who are still receiving education we find that the situation in the two villages 'P' and 'J' differs considerably. The pattern of difference we observed in respect of those who have already completed their education is maintained in case of those who are still receiving education.

In village 'P' the solitary student who has the distinction of studying the Bachelor's course in Engineering belongs to a Brahman family. Similarly both the post-graduate and all the 26 degree course students belong to Brahman caste. None of the students from either the Backward or the Scheduled caste or the non-Ashraf Muslim ethnic groups have the good fortune of going to postgraduate or degree classes. Again 35 out of a total of 37 students of the under-graduate classes are Brahmans, and of the remaining two one is a Jadav and the other a non-Ashraf Sheikh. In all the other levels the Brahman decisively predominate and for outnumber all the other groups taken together (Table 23).

In village 'J', however, the situation is very different. We do not find any student at the post-graduate level or studying in the technical institutions. But out of 9 students of the degree course, 3 belong to Ashraf, 4 to Jadav, 1 to Nonia and 1 to Dhobi caste. Similarly out of a total of 29 students in the category of VIII to X we find that 5 belong to Ashraf, 1 to non-Ashraf Sheikh, 9 to Jadav, 4 to Tanti, 1 to Gourhi, 8 to Nonia and 1 to Dhobi caste. In other categories also the Backward and Scheduled castes are fairly representad (Table 24).

Thus as we observed the two villages though unequal in area and the size of the population are not only in the same ecological setting but are also contiguous and adjacent to each other. In all matters relating to physical condition, topography, the quality and productivity of land. the system of irrigation they do not materially differ. Both the villages are governed by identical land tenure system and same agrerian laws. The social composition of the two villages differs only to the extent that village 'P' has traditionally been under lhe Zamindari of the Brahmans while village 'J' had been under the Zamindars belonging to the Sheikh Ashraf community. Besides the Brahmans and the Ashraf have been at the top of the traditional social hierarchy in the respective villages, the other groups in the two villages belonging to Backward and Scheduled Castes as

TABLE 21

Level of Education achieved by Castes and Ethnic Groups in Village 'P'

Sl. No.	Groups	No. of House-hold	No. of Indivi-dual	Illite-rate	Literate	Fducational Status									Total Educa-ted
						Upto Class III	IV-VIII	VIII-X	Passed S.F.	Upto under Gradu-ate	Gradu-ate	Post Gra-duate	Tech-nical/ Pro-fessio-nal	Other (Reli-gious)	
1.	Brahman	99	802	27	116	3	51	50	54	33	50	12	8	2	263 32.75
2.	Jadav	18	91	69	1										1 1.09
3.	Dhanuk	35	175	103	9		4	2	1						7 4.00
4.	Nai	13	76	42		2	5	4							11 4.44
5.	Tanti	65	360	227	10		5	2	7	2			1		14 3.88

6. Barhai	9	55	23	1			5	4	2					11 2.00
7. Dosadh	24	98	69	3		1	1	1						3 3.05
8. Chamar	30	128	86				2							2 1.56
9. Dom	6	26	8	7		1								
10. Mansoori	11	62	35	8			1	1						2 3.22
11. Sheikh	150	719	401	35	4	16	5	3					2	30 3 61
12. All Groups	460	2592	1090	192	7	77	76	75	37	50	12	9	4	345 13.31

TABLE 22

Level of Education achieved by Castes and Ethnic Groups in Village 'J'

Sl. No.	Groups	No. of House-hold	No. of Indivi-duals	Illiterate	Lite-rate	Educational Status: Upto Class III	IV-VIII	VIII-X	Passed S.F.	Upto Under Gra-duate	Gra-duate	Post Gra-duate	Tech-nical Pro-fessi-onal	Other (Reli-gious)	Total Educa-ted
1.	Sheikh Ashraf	24	118	9 7.62	32		1	12	8	4	5	1			31 26.27
2.	Sheikh	86	376	229 60.70	27		1		4	5	5				15 3.98
3.	Jadav	69	383	191 49.86	30	1	12	19	4	2	1	2			41 10.70
4.	Tanti	122	580	341 50.79	51	5	9	4	1		1				20 4.75
5.	Gourhi	17	98	49 50.00			4	6			1				11 11.22

6. Nonia	27	178	64 35.95	26		4	6	6				16 6.22
7. Barhai	2	14	3 21.42			1	2					3 21.42
8. Nai	7	37	28 75.67				1		1			1 5.28
9. Dosadh	19	95	66 69.47			1	2	3				6 6.31
10. Dhobi	9	50	14 28.00	4			5	3				8 5.55
11. All Groups	373	1929	994 51.12	170	6	33	57	29	12	13	3	

TABLE 23

Levels at which Education is Being Received by Castes and Communities in Village 'P'

Sl. No.	Groups	No. of House hold	Total Popu- lation	Illite- rates	Literate	Levels at which Receiving Education: Glass I-III	IV-VII	VIII-X	Under Gradu- ate	Gra- duate	Post Gra- duate	Tech- nical	Others	Total	
1.	Brahman	99	802	27	116	72	97	68	35	26	2	1*	1	301 37.53	*B.E.
2.	Jadav	18	91	69	1	2	1		1					4 4.39	
3.	Dhanuk	35	175	103	9	6	3	3						12 6.85	
4.	Nai	13	76	42	1	5	2	2						9 11.84	
5.	Tanti	65	360	227	10	13	7	6						26 7.22	

6. Barhai	9	55	23	2	10	2	3						15 27.27
7. Dosadh	24	98	69	3	2	3	1						6 6.12
8. Chamar	30	128	86		4	2	3						9 7.03
9. Dom	6	26	8	7	7		1						8 30.76
10. Mansoori	11	62	35	8	11								11 17.74
11. Sheikh	150	719	401	35	50	15	2	1				6+	74 10.29
12. All Groups	460	2592	1090	192	182	132	89	37	26	2	1	6	475 18.32

+Hafiz 3, Moulvi 2, Firqania 1

TABLE 24

Levels at which Education is Being Received by Castes and Communities in Village 'J'

Sl. No. Groups	No. of House hold	Total Popula-tion	Illiterate	Literate	Levels at which Receiving Education							Others	Total
					I-III	IV-VII	VIII-X	Under Gradu-ate	Gradu-ate	Post Gradu-ate	Tech-nical		
1. Sheikh Ashraf	24	118	9	32	8	9	5	8	3				33 27.96
2. Sheikh	86	376	229	27	5	8	1						14 3.72
3. Jadav	60	383	191	30	12	15	9	2	4				52 13.57
4. Tanti	122	580	341	51	26	14	4	4					48 8.27
5. Gourhi	17	98	49		10	2	1						13 13.26

6. Nonia	27	178	64	26	7	10	8	3	1	29 16.29
7. Barhai	2	14	3		1					4 28.57
8. Nai	7	37	28		2					2 5.40
9. Dosadh	19	95	66		3	1				4 4.21
10. Dhobi	9	50	14	4	12	2	1		1	16 32.00
11. All Groups	373	1929	994	170	88	62	29	17	9	215 11.14

well as non-Ashraf Muslim groups have had the tradition of occupying a status below them. 'P' has 11 and 'J' has 10 ethnic groups or castes, 5 of whom are common to both the villages. Six groups are exclusive to the former and 5 are exclusive to the latter. The five castes or ethnic groups, common to both the villages have kinship ties and marriage alliances.

The Brahman constitute 30.94 per cent of the total population of the village 'P' and 17.73 per cent of the combined population of the two villages. The Ashraf constitute 6·11 per cent of the total population of the village 'J' and 2·61 per cent of the combined population of the two villages. Brahmans dominate their village 'P' not only because of their numerical strength but also because of their ownership of land and the power and prestige they wield in the administrative network and the Government. The Ashraf on the other hand are under pressure from mainly the Backward castes who are numerically dominant.

While the Brahmans in Village 'P' have remained socially a closed group, strictly adhering to the caste norms of marriage and kinship, the Ashraf are relatively open and have caused the emergence of sub-groups as a result of marriage, in previous generations, with women of inferior social status, undermining the homogeneity of their group.

Both the Brahman and the Ashraf occupy the best and commanding positions in terms of space in their respective villages, their houses occupy larger areas than those of the houses of the members of other castes. Brahman houses are, however, better maintained and comprise a number of modern constructions. The houses of the Ashraf, with one or two exceptions, are in a state of decay and dilapidation, and give a desolate look.

In the layout of the village one will observe greater physical distance between the sectors occupied by the Brahmans and the sectors inhabited by the Scheduled castes. But Ashraf have not maintained physical distance with either the Backward or the Scheduled castes, and they live not only in close proximity but also interact in many ways without much of inhibition.

Traditionally both Brahmans of village 'P' and Ashraf of village 'J' have been landowners, but Brahmans have not allowed their land to go out of their castes, while large scaleland alienation has taken place in case of the Ashraf and the main beneficiaries are the Jadav and the Nonia of their village, as a result the members of these caste own more land than the Ashraf themselves.

It appears that the Brahmans of village 'P' have remained absolutely unconcerned about the problems of education and social development of the Backward and Scheduled castes of their village. It is not so in case of the Ashraf in village 'J'. The names of several members of this community are mentioned with gratitude by several members of the Backward castes in the village for active help and sympathies in their educational endeavour and employment at least until early forties. They did exercise their rights and privileges as Zamindars and land owners but were not adverse to the social developments of the Backward and Scheduled castes and in fact rendered assistance to them, somewhat selectively, in their educational endeavour. The establishment of a primary school in the village as early as mid thirties with a Nonia teacher from the village, mainly to cater to the needs of the Backward and the Scheduled caste children, owes to a member of the Ashraf community of the village. Another member of the Ashraf community who was the headmaster of a Middle School in a neighbouring village is known for encouraging the Jadav and Dhobi boys to receive education, some of whom hold prominent positions today. The present day condition of the Ashraf in the village does not justify similar expectations from them. Brahmans in village 'P' have not played similar roles in the past in respect of their Backward and Scheduled caste co-villagers nor there is any example of their endeavour in this regard.

One will fail to observe any voluntary endeavour on the part of the members of the upper castes, in the area of our study, for the educational or economic improvement of the lower castes. In fact no one appears to be actively interested in activities relating to the socio-cultural advancement of a caste other than his own. This is taken as a normal way of life. Any one among the forward caste who claims to have sympathies for the poor and the backward is not taken seriously by the latter.

Despite the fact that the Brahmans have deeper and more effective involvement with the network of administration and power than any other group in the area, and a large number of them have secured profitable jobs under the Government, in the Army and Air Force, in Scheduled Banks and organised secιor, besides receiving preferential treatment for jobs in commercial establishments of the Marwaris, their Backward and Scheduled caste co-villagers remain almost completely deprived of this benefit. Some of the members of the Backward and Scheduled castes in village 'J' have better achievement in matter of employment than not only their castemen in the other village but also the members of the Ashraf community in their own village. One of the reason for this achievement is their comparative educational advancement due largely to encouragement they received in the past from the advanced section of the village, though they have a lot to complain against the wider socio-political environment for lack of sympathy for their problems.

Thus we notice that the pattern of inter-caste relationship in a Brahman dominated village is characterised by a near perfect subordination and subserviance of the Backward and the Scheduled castes in matter of land ownership, literacy, education and in occupational pursuits. The perception of this situation on the part of the dominant and the dominated is pretty divergen .

The apparently apathetic attitude of the twice born towards the problems of socio-economic development of the lower castes and their 'equalisation' socially and economically, should not be misconstrued as something unusually antagonistic or hostile towards these unfortunate folk. Seen in the over all civilisational context this attitude is in fact consistent with the traditional pattern of beliefs and age-old practices which are in accord with the supposition that these 'low' caste people are to serve their overlords faithfully and ungrudgingly. The station of life they happen to be in is considered as unchangeable during their lifetime in any major way. The virtue on the part of these people is supposed, under this long established belief system, to lie in continuing to serve the twice born without aspiring to change their condition, and any attempt to do so is out-ragious, because it goes against the traditional social structure.

Any prospect of change in the social structure, seeking to alter the condition of the people that threaten to wean them away from the service they are supposed to render and place them in a position to compete their overlords is deemed not only directed towards undermining the structure but also against their interest. The psyche of the twice born caste and their mental framework as shaped by many thousands of years traditional beliefs and practices is thoroughly oriented towards non-acceptance of the philosophy of equality that encroaches upon the sphere of their prerogatives. The inner self of the twice born, at its sub-conscious level, is opposed to the idea that the Sudras should be equipped so that they begin competing them in spheres of activity that have come to be associated with them. This opposition is intellectually organised and deeply ingrained into the belief system based on the doctrine of *Karma* and *Dharma*,[1] though political exigencies and impact of modern ideas prevent them from verbalising their stand point. However, this organised feeling is translated into vield action to keep the underdog at the 'right' place. Though the system of stratification somewhat analogous to the system of caste is observable in the Muslim society, this has no religio-philosophical basis as we find in case of the Hindus.

The perception of the situation at the level of the Backward and Scheduled castes is somewhat different. Though they are also a part of the system of caste which assigns lower status to them and they have not only accepted this status passively, but have also applied the principles of superiority and inferiority in defining relationship among themselves. This remains fully

1. Caste and Political Recruitment in Bihar by Ramshray Roy in 'Caste in Indian Politics'. Ed. Rajni Kothari with reference to Iravati Karve, Hindu Society—An Interpretation, Poona, pp. 102-103.

valid even today, yet no sooner than they became aware of the rights and privileges granted to them under the new policy there has been a systematic accentuation of the feeling of deprivation and betrayal. The conflict in the caste society that was latent began getting manifest. In the village we have surveyed, we find the deprived castes entertaining a lot of grievances against the twice born, who are progressively appearing to them as those who have stood so long in the way of their progress and prosperity. These grievances are less vocal and suppressed when they have to face a formidable overlord. But in the village where the overlordship has disintegrated, the organised feeling works in a different direction, and keeps its supposed opponent under pressure, particularly when the erstwhile overlords do not figure significantly in the network of administration and power.

At the inter-community level there is a fair degree of involvement in social, economic and even certain ritual matters. The localities or even of residence in the villages, as we have observed earlier are segregrated but not distant from each other. The Brahman locality in village 'P' is however at fair distance from those of the Muslims as well as the Scheduled castes. The Ashraf in village 'J' do not maintain any significant distance from either the Backward Castes (Upper Sudras) or the Scheduled Castes (Lower Sudras).

The long habit of living together has not only resulted in complete mutual acceptability but also functional interdependence in many fields of socio-economic activities. Hindu barbers, washermen, and scavengers serve both Hindus and Muslims indiscriminately, so do carpenters and shoe makers. Muslim Mansoori not only do cotton carding but also supply mutton to both Hindus and Muslims.

Both the communities are segmentated on caste or beradari lines and a system of stratification is operative in both though in case of the Hindus it is ritually approved and has a religious significance, but in case of the Muslims it is not culturally approved.

The distinctiveness is visible in certain features of their beliefs and practices, food habits, nomanclature pattern yet their association with each other in a common habitat in close proximity and regular contact and in many cases their common origin and rootedness in the area have developed between them enough of understanding of each other. It is not unnatural to observe them sharing a lot of common superstitions, cherishing the same folk tales and devising similar methods of dealing with spirits and supernatural beings. Mutual respect for each other's shrines is a common feature. The shrine of Malek-ul-Ulema Mufti Ismail Danishmand at village 'J' popularly known as Dargah is held in reverence by the Hindus and is taken care of by a Jadav family. Muslims are observed approaching Gonu Baba Than, a place of worship of the Hindus, for cure of the cases of snake bites.

It is interesting to observe that barring a few orthodox people untouchability is fast disappearing from the village and members of both the communities eat and drink together indiscrimiminately on suitable occasions. Establishment of commensal relations across the community in the present society and village folk is a significant change that has occurred in recent years. This generally follows class line. 'Jal Chal' or 'Achal' norms, however, remain largely operative in case of the Brahmans though Brahmans do not normally refrain from offering food to Muslims of their class and also accepting food from them. Muslims no longer remain segregated or discriminated against in the matter.

In recent years political parties or their agents have been infiltrating in the villages to appoint local agents or to win support for themselves but very often it occurs in clandestien manner. This is because the villagers do not like to offend fellow villagers. This is particularly true in case of the partise who show bias against a particular community. This is quite significant because the social atmosphere in the villages is against preaching open disunity, and is attuned towards maintaining harmony. It is also significant that the tension along community lines ts not normally generated from local problems, they are largely the reflection of what is happening elsewhere in a wider area or at the national scene.

The perception of some kind of threat to the Muslim minority in the villages on account of the actiuities of external forces or their agents, howevcr clandestinely pursued, has its impact on the Muslim minority. They show a degree of co-hesiveness and develop a greater degree of solidarity among themselves. They being looking at the neighbouring Muslim vi lagers to devise methods for their protection and to meet the situation.

5

Political Development : Casteism and Communalism

An idea of the socio-economic life in some of the villages in the district of Bhagalpur, throwing considerable light on aspects of inter-caste relationship, could be had from the previous chapter. This provides a framework within which various castes and ethnic groups with their hopes and aspirations, deprivations and frustrations operate and go to shape the nature of socio-political developments in a wider area within which they are situated. The socio-political developments that are taking place in the district and the state or even in wider social environment embracing the nation are meaningfully intelligible to us in the context of what we observed in the villages.

We also noted considerable variations in the pattern of development in the two villages which had obviously a correlation with the nature of traditional social hierarchy, particularly at the top positions. This clearly brought home to us the importance of caste as a factor having a profound effect on the pattern of development in the role area of our observation. It will now be worthwhile to observe the role of caste in the society in a wider area in the wake of socio-political developments of the nature of political modernisation. This will facilitate our understanding of the process of caste consciousness developing into caste cleavages and confrontations and their over-all impact on tnter-group relations.

It must be remembered that the traditional social structure in India is organised on the basis of the caste system. This system has continued to operate in the Indian society from time immemorial setting its pattern of inter-relationship in thecultural, social, economic and political life of the Hindu society. Though as a pen-Indian phenomenon it has been observed to operate over a very wide area, it has regional and sub-regional systems, which while forming part of the same larger system, functions somewhat differently in different regions, depending upon a number of factors including the nature of social composition and economic pursuits at the local level. In certain regions some features of the caste are more rigidly adhered to than in others. As for example the ritual aspect of purity and pollution may be observed to be more rigid in Southern India where caste and social distance may appear to be of greater relevance than elsewhere.[1] Similarly economic disparity and unequal share in power and authority may be more glaring in some regions than probably in others, though ritual, economic, and political inequality may characterise the total system everywhere. system The of caste in India has its area of rigidity which we may call 'core area' while certain other areas may be less rigid in its observence. As for example caste in Assam may be less rigid than perhaps int he South and in the Gangetic valley.

Here we shall mainly confine ourselves to observe what shape political modernisation is taking in the caste oriented society or in other words how caste is reacting to political modernisation in the state of Bihar, setting patterns of inter-caste and inter-community relationship in the state.

1. Hutton reports the presence of caste of unseables in Tinnevally whose very sight polluted the upper castes. See Hutton's caste in India; 4th edition, p. 81. The names of castes like Tiyapad and Cherumapad indicating the number of steps they were supposed to be away from a member of the high caste. Hutton Op. Cit. p. 79.

The case factor coming into prominence in recent past has been attributed to government policies, such as the activisation of Kurmis and formation of 'Kurmi Mahasabha' towards the end of the last century in U.P. and later in Bihar. It is stated to be the result of their declaration as 'criminal caste', unfit for job in the armed forces (Verma-1974).[2] Risley's attempt at preparing in a list of Castes in 1901 according to their rank in society is stated by Mitra (1951)[3] to be another example of development of Caste consciousness through administrative action. But the phenomena of caste with all its attributes has always been present to attract attention. Its recording in the Census or similar other action by the government may have the effect of accelerating a process which already existed in the society.

It is true that the caste movement of the Kayasthas and the Bhumihars in Bihar began with the reform movement and the movement for educational and cultural uplift of the respective castes with the main object of gaining status in society and by virtue of their economic condition and cultural achievement, they came to be counted among the upper or forward castes. The origin of the involvement of Caste in politics can in no way be attributed to such government policies as stated by Verma (1974) or Mitra (1951). The nature of the involvement of caste in politics was probably inherent in the kind of organisation of the society characterised by the system of caste.

Several social analysists[4] trace the origin of caste cleavages to movements led by the Kayasthas of Bihar that resulted in

2. Verma, KK : 'Changing Role of Caste Association' A study of the Kurmi Mahasabha (referred to in Caste and Polititics in Bihar by H. Dhar and others in Land, Caste & Polities, ed. Gail Omvedt).
3. Mitra. A.. 'Tribes and Castes of Bengal', Census of India, 1951.
4. Vide for example (1) 'Caste & Political Recruitment in Bihar' by Ramshray Roy in Caste in Caste in Indian Politics, Ed. Rajni Kothari, Orient Longman, New Delhi; 1970. (2) 'Caste & Polity n Bihar' by H. Dhar and Others in 'Land, Caste & Politics in Indian States', Ed. G. Omvedt, Authors Guild Publication, Delhi 1982 and (3) 'Caste Politics in India, by Kiran Sukla, Mittal Publication, Delhi 1987; Pg. 25-50.

the separation of Bihar and Orissa from Bengal in 1912. It is said that Bengalis being among the earliest recepients of English education had virtually monopolised the white collar jobs in Bihar and the Kayasthas of Bihar who were among the first in the state to receive English education found it difficult to enter into the structure of opportunities because of Bengali domination. The movement with its slogan 'Bihar for Biharis, launched under the leadership of Sachidanand Sinha gained popularity, and with the formation of the new state in 1912 the Kayasthas of Bihar were immensely benefitted. They came to dominate the jobs and opportunities available to the natives in the newly formed province.

This movement, however, cannot justifiably be termed as a movement that gave rise to casteism in Bihar simply because it was led by the Kayasthas. Though it was not a mass movement and was led only by intellectuals, it was in fact a regional movement, directed mainly to strike a balance in the allocation of scarce resources which were unjustifiably eluding the grasp of the local people, who legitimately deserved the same. The Kayasthas, however, being the earliest in Bihar to receive English education, held virtual monopoly of the government jobs or entered into the white collar jobs in a massive way in the newly formed state. This became possible on account of the "domicile rule" which was enacted to prevent people from outside the state to secure jobs in Bihar. But as other forward castes of Bhumihars and Rajputs and later Maithil Brahmans, who were numerically significant and economically better off, acquired English education, they came in the field to contest for positions and power. The monopoly of the Kayasthas was thus challenged. It is significant that the caste was utilised by all the parties concerned as an instrument to organise their respective groups for the achievement of their goals in the political and economic fields. The process of political modernisation was systematically opening up new avenues, though until ninteen-twenties, the goals were limited to representation in municipal and district boards and in white collar jobs and later in legislatures, constituted under the Act of 1935.

This process of limited democratisation and an urge to participate in the same activised castes on a scale unknown in the past. This involved political mobilisati on ofthe caste by caste elitis in their own interest Commenting on the situation O'Melley[5] writes "It is disappointing to find that candidates for election to the legislature solicit the votes of their caste men simply on the strength of their caste fellowship without regard to caste considerations (1932 : 182).

Thus the involvement of caste in politics became conspicuous with the introduction of political reform and formation of responsible government in the state. Its main objective has been to strive for acquiring more and more power for ones' own caste and similarly depriviug other castes from gaining strength in the spheres of politics and new avenues of economy or employment. This sometimes involved alliances between various castes as against others, as for example between Kayasthas and Rajputs against Bhumihars and between Kayasthas and Bhumihars against Rajputs and Brahmans.

In the early phase of the introduction of political modernisation until early sixties, the inter-caste rivalry and competition for wresting power and position for ones' own caste, within the frame-work of opportunities, characterised only the four upper or forward castes namely the Kayasthas, Bhumihars, Rajputs and Brahmans. Political leadership drawn from these castes is alone observed endeavouring to compete with each other for political gains. They occasionally drew support from the backward and scheduled castes i.e., the upper and the lower Sudras in their struggle for power, but by and large the struggle remained confined to upper castes mainly for the benefit of upper castes (Mishra – 1986 : 23).

The non-participation of weak participation of the upper and the lower Sudras in the struggle for wresting power in the initial stages of political modernisation was due to various factors including the low level of their aspiration on account of backwardness and traditional passivity. They generally lacked an attitude of aggressive self-assertion. The movements of these castes generally characterised social mobility mevements.

5. O'Melley, L.S.S. Indian Caste Customs, 1943.

to gain status and greater respectability in the hierarchically ordered Hindu society. They had established a number of caste sabhas or associations for the purpose.[6] These caste sabhas of the upper and lower Sudras mainly functioned in the sphere of social reform and with rare exception they operated on a model of 'Sanskritization'. They did not work to compete overtly the upper castes to wrest political power from them, though these movements may be interpreted as a struggle for achieving higher status and perhaps social equality, which remained as a distant goal. Thus it was much later that the so called backward and scheduled castes joined the struggle for a better deal for themselves in the structure of power and opportunities that were opened up on account of political modernisation.[7]

Since Kayasthas had spearheaded the movement for the separation of Bihar and Orissa from Bengal and they constituted the educated class,[8] they were immensely benefitted by the creation of a large number of posts in the newly formed state. Their dominance in white collar jobs provoked jealousies among other upper castes mainly the Bhumihars and Rajputs who because of their socio-economic condition soon acquired education. Their numerical strength also gave them added advantage over the Kayasthas. The latter consciously endeavoured to preserve their position and power. This situation brought caste rivalries to the fore.

6. The caste Sabhas of the Yadav, Kurmi and Koiri, the tenant castes extended their activities somewhat beyond the scope of 'Sanskritization' ond occasionally took action to protect their right as tenents against the Rajput and Bhumihar land lords.

7. The eole of Kisan Sabha formed in 1328 and such organisation as Triveni Sangh and Backward Caste Federat on in developing consciousness of their rights was quite considerable.

8. Constituting less than 2% of the population of the state the Kayastha students in the under-graduate class of the Patna College figured 30% in 1936 while all the four upper castes taken together eonstituted 70% of the total strength of the students in the same class (Vide 'Caste and Political Recruitment in Bi2ar, by Ramshray Roy).

The formation of responsible government in 1937 under the Act of 1935 brought to light rivalries and infighting within the Congress between S.K. Sinha and A.N. Sinha belonging to Bhumihar and Rajput castes respectively. The struggle for leadership of the Assembly party as such was not unusual in a democracy, but what gave it a caste colour was their utilisation of their respective caste in their support. S.K. Sinha, however, became the Chief Minister. The question of leadership re-emerged in 1946 but, with the intervention of the high command, was resolved in favour of S.K. Sinha.

Among the major pre-occupations of the Congress as a national party in Bihar on the eve of the first general elections were the distribution of tickets to candidates for central and state legislatures and selection of Chief Minister. The behaviour of the two main sub-coalitions within the party, dominated by the Bhumihar and the Rajput respectively, openly demonstrated their bias in favour of their respective castes. There were open accusations of casteism to the extent that both these factions had descended to the level of supporting their caste men against their party candidates. The story of A.N. Sinha aiding a Rajput candidate to unseat S.K. Sinha and of K.B. Sahay working for the defeat of Vinodananda Jha a party candidate gained wide currency (Sukhla—1987 : 38). It was also noticed that the Chief Minister ignored his non-Bhumihar supporters like Sarangdhar Singh, a Rajput and K.B. Sahay, a Kayastha and pushed up the case of M.P. Sinha, a less prominent leader of his own caste, who seriously involved himself in campaign against the non-Bhumihar supporters of the Chief Minister, spousing the cause of his castemen. K.B. Sahay who was earlier weaned away by the Chief Minister from his alliance with the Rajput faction went back to their fold in protest.

The struggle between various caste factions within the Indian National Congress was not based on policies and programmes to any significant extent because they all pursued, by and large a policy of preserving the socio-economic status-quo and the structure of the society, not allowing the privileges, the upper castes enjoyed, to be reduced. It was a struggle of various upper castes to enjoy power and to distribute it among their own caste men and no more.

Casteism mainly in the arena of sharing, rather holding in full control, of power continued to grow. The participants in the game were mainly the upper castes. This on the eve of the second general elections manifested itself in all out endeavour on the part of each caste to obtain maximum number of nominations for its own members. Morarji Desai had to settle the difficult problem. Cases of leaders campaigning against party members in support of their caste men again came to limelight.

With the death of both S.K, Sinha and A.K. Sinha in ealy sixties there were three main aspirants of Chief Ministership namely K.B. Sahay, M.P. Sinha and B.N, Jha, belonging to Kayastha, Bhumihar and Maithil Brahman Castes. B,N. Jha became the Chief Minister with the support of K.B. Sahay for the remaining period. K.B. Sahay, however, shifted his loyalty to his arch rival M.P. Sinha.

The problem of allocation of tickets to candidates assumed unprecedented complications in 1962. The Pradesh Election Committee shifted to Delhi but it also failed to come to a final conclusson and the problem was finally resolved with the personal intervention of Late. Sm, Indira Gandhi. B.N. Jha became the Chief Minister to be Kamrajed in 1963.

It was for the first time during the tenure of the third State Assembly that the case of a Kurmi leader, Birchand Patel for the post of Chief Ministership was spoused by B.N. Jha, the outgoing Chief Minister. Though Birchand did not succeed in getting the post, this aroused enthusiasm and later frustation among the backward castes and they began seriously thinking of climbing the ladder and wresting the coveted position, through capturing more seats in the Assembly.

Until the third general elections Congress had continued to remain a dominant national political party commanding absolute majority in the State Assembly. It was a stronghold of the upper castes and the struggle for leadership and inter-caste rivalries for capturing political power had remained confined to the upper castes. As a result of the 1962 elections its strength had reduced from 210 to 185 and a number of small parties had emerged. Swatantra Party (50) was the largest among them. The Praja Socialist Party with its strength of 29 members was the third largest party in the Assembly, followed by the Communist parties having 12 members while Jana Sangh had returned three members. A new trend of the nature of polarisation of economic interests became visible, though crystallisation of economic issues were not sharp and persistent and whenever came to the fore were ineffective. The membership of the backward castes had increased from 22.86 per cent in 1957 to 30.50 per cent in 1962. Birchand Patel's failure resulted in developing a sense of solidarity among the backward castes. They started coming closer to each other to achieve their objective of getting a better deal for their castemen. Several leaders of the backward castes like Ram Lakhan Jadav and Deve Saran Singh came into prominence.

The fourth general election was of great significance. The results showed that the backward and the scheduled castes had gained consciousness to the extent unknown in the past. Congress mainly a party dominated by the upper castes was reduced to 128 in the house of 319 members. Several political parties emerged which were almost exclusively confined to backward and scheduled castes, S.S.P., a party of the upper Sudras, namely the Jadav, the Kurmi and the Koeri emerged as the second largest party securing 68 seats in the Assembly. The ever increasing strength of the backward castes was a matter of concern for the upper castes because it posed a potential threat to their privileged position and the conservative elements of the upper castes as also the trading castes responded in several ways which include greater support to Hindu Communal organisation, namely the Jana Sangha. It is significant that in this election Jana Sangha captured 26 seats, recorda number so far. A conscious and deliberate communalisation of the socie'y would obviously appear to have a correlation with greater consciousness among the backward and Scheduled castes and a demand on their part to have a due share in the structure of power and opportunities in the State. Thus a section of the upper caste teltles who were largely responsible for introducing castism in politics get disiillusioned by the growing consciousness among are backward and Harijan castes and started drifting towards communalism to forget unity in the caste society.

After the first coalition ministry led by M.P. Sinha fell under the pressure of the backward castes, two successive ministeries were formed under the leadership of B.P. Mondal, a Shastri, leader of backward caste and later under Bhola Paswan a scheduled caste leader, but these were also short lived and caste conflicts mainly involving upper and backward castes made the formation of a stable government impossible. This led to the dissolution of the Assembly and the establishment of the President's rule in the state.

The results of the mid-term poll in 1969 instead of reversing the trend accelerated the pace of the emergence and growth of smaller parties and the number of parties in the Assembly almost doubled itself reducing the Congress to 118 in the House of 319 an all time low so far. The combined strength of the Communist parties remained constant (28) but the Jana Sangh increased its number from 26 to 34. The lower castes, though represented by several parties like S.S.P., P.S.P., Soshist Dal, B K.D. etc., taken together improved their position considerably. An experiment in the formation of government under the leadership of Sardar Harihar Singh, a Scheduled caste Chief Minister failed in only a few month's time due to opposition from another Scheduled caste leader Bhola Paswan Shastri, who replaced him but he could not survive himself more than a couple of months. President's rule was clamped for the second time. Later Daroga Prasad Rai, Karpoori Thakur and Bhola Paswan Shastri, all belonging to lower castes held the post of Chief Ministership and this boosted the morale of the backward and scheduled castes to a considerable extent, but at the same time the ephimeral character of their governments had a frustating effect on the people in general.

The sixth general election that took place in 1972 after the Congress government's triumph in Bangladesh in an exceptionally changed mood in the country, improved the strength of the Congress party in the state from 118 to 167, though the party's strength could not reach the level of the first three general elections. The Chief Ministership during this tenure of the Assembly was shared successively by Kedar Pande, Abdul Ghafoor and Jagannath Mishra. The backward castes lay almost low, because victory over Pakistan achieved by the Congress government at the centre had given tremendous boost to the Congress party including its unit in the state and had crowned it with victory. The later phase of the tennure was however unusually stromy on account of the declaration of internal emergency and alleged subversion of democracy in the country.

The seventh general election in 1977, fought on the issue of democracy versus authoritarian rule, pushed the ruling party into extreme insignificance. It could secure only 57 seats in the house of 325 members. It was a period of the Janata wave, which had a tremendous support of the backward castes as also of the extreme right. The Janata Party secured 214 seats and almost all the smaller parties excepting the two communist parties got merged with Janata. The Jana Sangh got tremendous amount of respectability by merging itself with the Janata Party and the J.P. Movement. Tactically this served the party well. The members drawn from backward castes constituted a majority in the Janata Assembly party in the state and Karpoori Thakur the respected leader of the backward caste formed the government.

So far the politics of the backward castes was mainly directed towards increasing their strength by capturing larger number of seats in the Assembly and securing ministerial posts. Their leaders belonging mainly to rich peasant class, had not concentrated their efforts to uplift their caste economically or take ameleorative measures for their benefit in any significant way. Now when they had the political power in their hands they took some measures for their benefit. One of the measures related to the implementation of the policy of 'reservation' for the backward castes. This led to upheavals on a scale hitherto unknown. The divide between the forward and backward castes became sharper and the upper castes clearly rallied behind the Congress and the J.S. and became united to oppose the reservation policy of the Karpoori Thakur government. The two year rule of the

TABLE 25

Party Position in Bihar Legistative Assembly from 1952 to 1989[9]

S. No.	*Parties*	*1952*	*1957*	*1962*	*1967*	*1969*	*1972*	*1977*	*1980*	*1985*	*1989*
1.	Congress	239	210	185	128	118	167	57	175	193	71
2.	Socialist	23	2	7	—	—	34	—	—	—	1
3.	Jharkhand-J.M.M.-H.J.	33	32	20	—	7	8	1	11	9	20
4.	Janata	11	23	—	—	15	—	214	55	15	3
5.	L.S.Sangh	7	—	—	—	—	—	—	—	—	—
6.	Praja Socialist	1	31	29	18	18	—	—	—	—	—
7.	F.B. (M)	1	—	—	—	—	—	1	1	—	—
8.	Parishad	1	—	—	—	—	—	—	—	—	—
9.	CPI-C.P. (M)	—	7	12	28	28	35	25	29	13	29
10.	Jana Sangh-B.J.P.	—	—	5	26	34	25	—	20	16	39
11.	Swatantra	—	—	50	3	3	—	—	—	—	—
12.	S.S.P.	—	—	—	68	53	—	—	—	—	—

13. L.T.Cong.	—	—	—	—	9	—	—	—	—	—
14. B.K.D.	—	—	—	—	6	—	—	—	—	—
15. Cong.(O)	—	—	—	—	—	30	—	—	—	—
16. J.K.D.	—	—	—	26	—	—	—	—	—	—
17. Soshit Dal	—	—	—	—	6	2	—	—	—	—
18. Lok Dal	—	—	—	—	—	—	—	—	46	—
19. Cong (U)	—	—	—	—	—	—	—	13	—	—
20. SUCI	—	—	—	—	—	—	—	—	1	—
21. J.D.	—	—	—	—	—	—	—	—	—	122
22. Ind. People's Front	—	—	—	—	—	—	—	—	—	7
23. Marxist Coordination Party	—	—	—	—	—	—	—	—	—	2
24. Ind. Cong (SO)	—	—	—	—	—	—	—	—	1	—
25. Independent	14	11	—	21	22	16	25	18	29	30
26. Others	—	2	12	—	—	—	—	—	—	—
27. Nominated	—	1	1	1	1	1	1	1	1	1
28. Vacant	—	—	—	—	1	1	1	4	3	—
Total	330	319	319	319	319	319	325	325	325	325

9. *Source*: According to figures published by Director Secretariate, Bihar Patna.

Thakur government experienced violent protests, wanton destruction of the government property and virulent caste riots. The situation did not change in any significant measures when Ram Sunder Das came to occupy the chair of Chief Mininstership for a brief period of less than a year. President's rule was imposed for the fifth time in the state preceding the 8th general election, which in the wake of Janata experiment pushed the parties supported by the backward castes somewhat in the background. The unrest among the backward on handling the issues like reservation as also the land reform and agrarian problems were quite manifest, The unrest often took the shape of caste conflicts in several areas of the state.

The general elections in 1985 was immensely influenced by a wave of sympathy on account of the assasination of Sm. Indira Gandhi. Both the 8th and 9th Assemblies were dominated by the Congress and the politics of the backward Castes remained somewhat in a low key though the unrest among them remained smouldering beneath the surface. The general election of 1989 however brought the parties supported by the backward castes in a comfortable position in the State Assembly. This happened despite the fact that political parties supported by the upper castes particularly the extreme rightists like the BJP had tried to communalise the atmosphere endeavouring to forge inter-caste unity with the object of gaining political power by disarming the deprived section of society namely the backward and scheduled castes.

The onward march of the backward and scheduled castes in securing better representation in the elected bodies was already evident from the panchayat elections in 1972, the last to be held in Bihar (Vide Table 27). There may be a variety of reasons for not holding panchayat elections after 1972, but it is widely believed that since the backward castes had swep tthe polls in 1972 and are almost certain to repeat their performance rather improve their position, the elections have been kept abeyance.

A systematic increase in the representation of the backward and scheduled castes in the State Legislature right from 1952 (Vide Table 26) may not be a correct index of the increase of 'contest' type of leadership among the communities as against 'sponsored'[10] ones, because those elected were also representing various political parties with varied ideologies and programmes, yet this increase in number and proportion is definitely the index of political consciousness among them. A kind of leadership among the backward castes also emerged which had its base in the backward castes, particularly since Karpoori Thakur came to occupy the position as Chief Minister or as a leader of opposition.

A number of problems such as those relating to agrerian relation, implementation of rational minimum wages, strict implementation of the laws relating to bonded labour, reservation of jobs as well as seats in the Legislative Assembly etc., were of vital interest to the deprived sections of the society, yet the issue that caused serious differences between the upper and the lower castes was the problem of reservation. Karpoori Thakur's attempt to implement the Janata Party manifesto relating to reservation in government jobs for the backward castes in March 1979 led to serious conflicts. The policy on reservation was in line with the report of the Backward Class Commission headed by Kaka Kalekar submitted in 1955. Karpoori Thakur tried to implement the policy of seat reservation in the legislative assembly for the backward castes, but this accelerated the process of polarisation of the forward and backward castes into opposite camps. The upper castes were very much enraged and agitated. There was considerable disaffection among the more backward castes such as Tanti, Dhanuk, Banpar, Gangota, Nai, Kanu etc. So the 23 per cent reservation of he Government jobs were decided to be divided among the backward and more backward castes in a way that 8 per cent was reserved for Kotri, Kurmi, Bania and Jadav while 12 per cent was reserved for Tanti, Dhanuk, Banpar, Nai, Kanu etc. 14 per cent was already reserved for the scheduled castes, 2 per cent for

10. 'Contest' leadership are those which emerge from with n group while 'sponsored' ones are nominated by groups outside ones own. This concept has been used by R.A. Shermerhorn in 'Minorities in India : A Quantative Approach' (Main Currents in Indihn Sociology: Vol. III (Ed.) Giriraj Gupta Vikas Pub. House; New Delhi—1978).

TABLE 26

Caste Composition of MLAs from 1957 to 1985

	Percentage of Caste Groups							
Caste Groups	*1957*	*1962*	*1967*	*1969*	*1972*	*1977*	*1980*	*1985*
Forward	44.25	59.00	53.00	53.90	54.80	48.60	31.07	36.07
Backward	22.86	30.50	34.50	34.60	29.50	37.00	35.38	29.62
SCIST	17.62	1.70	2.90	2.50	2.00	4.90	23.38	23.76
Muslims	11.43	8.80	7.40	7.60	13.20	10.00	8.92	10.18
Others	3.80		2.20	1.70			1.25	
Total	99.96	100.00	100.00	100.00	99.50	100.50	99.90	99.53

Source: Figure up to 1977 from Caste Politics in India by Kiran Shukla, the rest from "Ashtam Bihar Vidhan Sabha" & "Navam Bihar Vidhan Sabha" published by the Director Secretariate, Printing Press, Bihar, Patna.

TABLE 27

Representation of Castes/Ethnic Groups in 16 Panchayats of Jagdishpur Block Constituted in 1972

Sl. No.	*Group*	*Sarpanch*	*Sarpanch & his Cabinet*	*Mukhia*	*Mukhia & his Cabinet*	*Total Strength*
1.	Forward Castes	2 (12.50)	8 (6.61)	2 (12.50)	13 (9.92)	
2.	Backward Castes	9 (56.26)	65 (53.71)	9 (56.25)	68 (51.90)	
3.	Scheduled Castes	1 (6.25)	16 (13.22)		19 (14.50)	
4.	Muslims	4 (25.00)	32 (26.44)	5 (31.25)	31 (23.66)	
5.	All Groups	16 (100.00)	121 (100.00)	16 (100.00)	131 (100.00)	

Notes : Figures in bracket are the per cent.

female and 2 per cent for poor members of the high caste. This was supposed to be with regard to all jobs in the whole of the state, but a modification of the decision during the subsequent Congress rule took place and it was not applied in the districts i.e., jobs and vacancies in the district administration as well as those of teachers in the district were excluded from the purview of reservation.[11] The leaders of the backward caste were very much agitated on what they thought a gross violation of the decision by the successors of Karpoori Thakur, The inter-caste relationship was never so tense as now and the upper and the lower caste groups were almost on open confrontation. Inter-caste conflicts became frequent.

Caste Conflicts

Caste conflicts in Bihar in the past had been latent rather than manifest. The earliest manifestation of conflict in 1921-25 both in North and South Bihar villages was the disastrous impact of the Permanent Settlement (1793) of the British Colonialist that had resulted in the socio-economic opression of the peasantery, mainly belonging to backward castes by the landowners largerly belonging to the upper castes. The systematic improvrishment of the peasants had by that time reached a point that could not be endured. Thus the conflict that became manifest in twenties was on both counts, economic and social, including the attempt on the part of the backward castes to wear sacred thread.[12] But the conflict in the form it is taking place is somewhat a new phenomenon. The frequency intensity and magnitude of caste riots as it is today has no parallel in history. This has obviously a direct correlation with the process of social change induced by democratisation or political modernisation. It is not possible here to give the detailed account of each and every incident of caste violence that has occured in Bihar in recent years. We shall present here merely a list of some incidents during the last decade that have taken place in the state.

11. Sri Jogeshwar Mondal, Ex. Minister; Govt. of Bihar in a personal interview in 1988.
12. Vide Hetukar Jha; Caste Conflict in Bihar, in the Times of India, May 5, 1978.

Some Recent Caste Conflicts in Bihar

Sl. No.	*Year*	*Area*	*Nature of Conflict*
1	2	3	4
1.	March 1977	Karghar Block of Rohtas District.	Upper caste landlords attacked Harijans who were demanding higher wages.
2.	June 1977	Gopalpur	Upper caste landlords attacked Harijans, their women were molested, because they were demanding higher wages.
3.	June 1977	Patahara, Bhagalpur	36 men and women from amongst the labourers were confined to a school building and brutally assaulted.
4.	Oct. 1977	Bharampara	4 share croppers belonging to lower castes were killed by upper caste landlord for demanding occupancy rights.

1	2	3	4
5.	1978	Belchi	11 Harijans were burnt alive by Kurmi landowners.
6,	1979	Monger	A village cobbler was killed by Kajput landlord.
7.	June 1979	Village : Samahara, Rohtas	4 Harijans were killed by some Rajputs as a result of a long standing land disputs.
8.	Feb. 1980	At Pipra, Patna District	200 Kurmis invaded a Harijan village. 27 houses of the Harijans were burnt a 3 year child was thrown into fire. 14 Harijans including 5 women and 6 children were killed.
9.	1980	Parasbigha	11 Yadavs were killed by upper castes.
10.	May, 1983	Dohia, Jahanabad	10 Bhumihars were killed by members of the lower caste.
11.	1983	Deoria, Jahanabad	5 Bhumihars and 1 Harijan were killed in a caste riot.

1	2	3	4
12.	Oct. 1983	Bapubigha, Nalanda.	Upper caste people of the neighbouring village gang raped Harijan women, plundered their locality because the Harijans had declined to play the musical band since they had previous contract elsewhere.
13.	May 1985	Madanganj, Jahanabad	CPI activist were killed in retaliation to the killing of 8 upper caste men including Mukhia a few weeks ago. It was a sequel to Bhumihar – Jadav tussle over job reservation.
14.	1986	Village : Darmia	Rajputs were killed in clash with Jadava – Operation elimination was ordered by C.M.
15.	1987	Choti Chechani	Rajputs clashed with Jadav and killed some of them.

1	2	3	4
16.	1987	Village : Dalelchak and Badhaura, Aurangabad	Jadavs massacred Rajputs in retaliation to the incident at Choti Chechani.
17.	1987	Hunterganj and Pratappur, Hazaribagh	Harijans organised a dharna against Zamindar who was forcefully occupying and ploughing their land. The police fired on the Harijans.
18.	1988	Village ; Jalim, Palamau	Clash between Sahu and Rajputs. Rajpu had detained a Sahu boy for interrogation which infuriated the Sahus and they attacked the Rajputs. Rajputs retaliated, burnt Sahu houses and killed seven of them and injured a dozen.
19.	1989	Jahanabad and Rohtas	Armed gangs of several castes killed each other. A family of five belonging to Brahman caste were killed allegedly by Harijans as a revenge.

20.	1991	Pipra and Sindeswar, Sahara	400 Harijan huts were set on fire by members of the upper castes as a result of land dispute.

Sl. No. 1 to 8 : P.R. Rajgopal—"Social Change and Violence : The Indian Experience". pp. 90–97.
Sl. No. 9 : P.R. Rajgopal—"Social Change and Violence : The Indian Experience".
Sl. No. 10 : Vide Times of India, May 28, 1983; referring to previous occurrence.
Sl. No. 11 :
Sl. No. 12 : Times of India ; Oct. 11, 19[illegible]3.
Sl. No. 13 : Times of India, May 28, 1985.
Sl. No. 14 : Vide Times of India, Bombay ; June 3 and 10 ; 1987 report.
Sl. No. 15 : Op. Cit,
Sl. No. 16 : Op. Cit.
Sl. No. 17 : Amrita Bazar Patrika, Oct. 24, 1987.
Sl. No. 18 : Hindustan Times, New Delhi ; May 25, 1988.
Sl. No. 19 : The Statesman : Jan. 4, 1989 and Amrita Bazar Patrika, Jan. 12, 1989.
Sl. No. 20 : Times of India ; March 2, 1991.

These are but a few examples of the caste conflicts in various parts of Bihar which would run into hundreds during a short span of a decade. The decision to implement the Mandal Commission's recommendation for reserving 27.00 per cent of the jobs for the socially and economically backward classes at the national level has virtually the effect of setting the country on fire. Its impact on Bihar has been enormous, and the polarisation between the forward and backward castes seems to be almost complete and perhaps decisive. The forward castes argue that the idea of reservation is opposed to (1) a merit based system and that (2) it rekindles the 'dying' members of casteism in the Indian society and unleashes a caste war which is so disastrous for the country. The issue has so much emotionalised the younger gsnerations that several cases of self-immolation has been reported from different parts of the country.

The pro-reservationists which besides the backward castes include several intellectuals, journalists and politicians from a cross section of the Indian society try to ask the question whether the present system of education and employment is based on equal opportunity and whether merit has been a basic criterian in making educational and employment opportunities available to various segments of our population? Is a few small steps to rectify the error of the denial of participatory democracy to a decisively large chunk of the population, identified as a backward caste, tantamount to a caste war? Hundreds of arguments and counter argument based on these basic questions are being put forth and the debate has been virulent and inconclusive. In the meanwhile the tension has been mounting and the battle is being fought politically not unmixed with violence.

Hindu-Muslim Conflict

Hindus and Muslims, as observed in the villages do operate as distinct communities, yet their centuries old association in a common habitat has developed among them enough of under-standing of each other. This has led to mutual adjustment of their behaviour. Mutual acceptance characterises their attitude in the villages and mutual functional inter-dependence is visible in their behaviour. They share many cultural features including local dialect and local beliefs and superstitions. The divergence in their respective cultures has seldom come in the way of their intimate relationship. They have developed mechanism to resolve the problems of living together and have traditionally lived peacefully in their common habitat. Having a look at the tradition of co-operation and harmony that has characterised their life at least until a few years ago one would have ruled out the possibility of emergence of tension and conflict leading one to destroy the other.

One will still be justified if he rules out such a possibility by drawing his conclusions through limiting his observation to the villages and ignoring the impact of developments in the wider area namely the state and the country.

Developments outside the micro region are however of vital importance, because they determine a good deal the nature of relationship between the two communities in a situation that prevails today. The issues that determine inter-community relationship are not local, they are broad based and concern the whole of the state and the country. Many of the issues that plague inter-community relationship are not of contemporary origin but have been dug out and have the elements of retrospection.

Anti-Muslim riots have become so frequent and so widespread in the country that they have a deadening effect on the soul and have stopped pricking the conscience. People in general are no longer alarmed over their occurrences as they used to be a decade or so ago. Instead of expressing shame over the deliberate destruction of innocent lives, the authorities are often observed to be boastful over the non-occurrence of communal violence for a considerable period as though something extraordinary and unnatural has been made to happen. The victims often allege the hands of those in the riots who were expected to restore and maintain peace.

Here we shall briefly describe the Bhagalpur riot that took place in October 1989 just when data for this write up was being collected. Bhagalpur is one of the 55 places, spread across 9 states where communal riots broke out in the 10 weeks preceding the Lok Sabha elections. Ram Shila processions became the immediate cause in most of the places. It was the largest Hindu-Muslim riot in the district since 1947, which eclipsed the carnage at Moradabad, Jamshedpur, Ahmedabad and other parts of Gujarat, Meerut, Maliana, Hashimpura, Bihar Sharif, Indore and a thousand such places in severity, intensity and magnitude. It surpassed many records of brutality that man has subjected to his fellow men.

The whole area, both towns and villages, were tense for several weeks before the actual conflict as the consecrated bricks were carried from villages to towns particularly to Bhagalpur city to be ultimately carried to Ayodhya in U.P. for laying the foundation of a Ramjanam Bhoomi temple on the sight of a mosque known as Babri Masjid. After minor skirmished in the suburban village of Fatehpur in Sabaur Block on 22nd and 23rd of October 1989 a major conflict started in the city where convergence of Ramshila procession took place and as the processionists insisted on passing through predominantly Muslim locality shouting abusive and provocative slogans[13] the conflict took place. In the city loot, plunder, killing and arson continued almost unchecked until 31st of October when para military forces established some semblance of order, though not peace and tranquility.

Communal violence spread to rural areas on 25th of October where armed mobs destroyed over 272 villages often rendering their inhabitants homeless ond killing many of them.

In the city some of the Muslim localities affected were Naya Bazar, Parbati, Noorpur, Jogsar, Sahibyanji, Moshaekhchak, Madani Nagar, Ishaqchak, Qazichak, Shakrullah Chak, Mir Ghias Chak, Makhsoospur, Khanjarpur, Mojahidpur, while

13. Some of the slogans raised by the processionists were ;

(a) Garbh Se Kaho Hum Hindu Hain,

(b) Yadi Is Desh Mein Rahna Hoga To Hindu Ban Ke Rahna Hoga,

(c) Babar Ki Aulad, Mohammad Ki Aulad, Bharat Choro,

(d) Jai Maa Kali Tatoapur Karo Khali.

137 Muslim shops in the main Shujaganj Bazar were looted and burnt.

In the village Logain most of its inhabitants were killed and put in a couple of mass graves over which cauliflower were quickly sown, their houses were burnt, while in village Chanderi most of the inhabitants were butchered ond thrown in the pool. Some of the worst affected Muslim villages were Salampur, Noorpur, Tamauni, Chakbir, Bhaturia and Russalpur.

It is estimated that over 1,05,000 individuals were affected, 35,000 people were rendered homeless and had in most cases to be shifted to places of safety. Over 6,000 houses were burnt, 3,000 houses in other villages were completed looted, 891 shops were looted or burnt. About 1,000 dead bodies have been recovered which include 42 non-Muslims. 42 mosques, 10 graveyards, 9 madrasas, 6 Imambaras have been dessroyed either fully or partially.

The most significant aspect of the Bhagalpur riots in 1989 is that tension persisted long after the catastroph in October and November and no notable endeavour was made by political leaders to defuse the tension. This was obviously due to the desire on their part to utilise the tension for their political interest, particularly during the eve of the general elections.

The brutality displayed in the riots would probably show that Hindus in the area were harbouring extreme hatred against their Muslim neighbours, but it will be wrong to draw such a hasty conclusion. Much of the misconceptions will disappear once we learn about (1) the enormous sum of money collected by the business community for the purpose, (2) a large number of criminals and ruffians were brought on hire from the neighbouring areas including the northern part of the district so well known for their criminality and brutal behaviour, (3) the promise of proteetion made to murderers and plunderers, (4) the inducement and alluration to certain weaker sections of society for enjoying the looted property, (5) the role of certain politicians in either organising the conflict laboriously or of some others in appeasing the sentiments so carefully worked up on the Ramjanam Bhoomi—Babri Masjid issue, (6) the role of the mass media particularly of some Hindi newspapers brazonly spreading false and wild rumours and (7) above all the questionable behaviour of influential political leaders and administrators.

It is true that a kind of general apathy on the part of the neighbours in an overall communalised atmosphere did not allow to develop sufficient resistance against the brutal acts, but joint resistance against riators and mutual pledge by Hindu and Muslim co-villagers to maintain peace was not altogether absent.

Muslim practice of polygyny, disproportionate increase in their population, their opposition to any attempt at homogenisation of their personal law, resurgence of fundamentalism in some Islamic countries and the creation of Pakistan are some of the reasons put fortth by some people for Hindu communalism. These people were found to be unware of the fact that according to a very broad based survey of the incidence of polygyny among several communities, Mnslims were found to be least polygynous.[14] They did not know that the procreative behaviour of a class, irrespective of the religious community, is identical and the community that has a larger concentration of people below the poverty line is likely to have a higher breeding rate due to socio-economic factors including the labour value of children. Also the mortality rate among the category of people is higher. They also do not appreciate that the anxiety of a cultural minority for its cultural preservation is not unexpected particularly in the wake of an onslaught from the dominant majority. It is also not understood how Muslims in India can exercise control over conntries like Iran, Saudi Arabia or some other countries where Islamic fundamentalism in believed to have gained

14. Vide Census of India 1961, 'Incidence of Polygynous Marriages in India', Office of the Registrar General, India, Ministry of Home Affairs, New Delhi—110011. Based on a census of 587 villages and 99,457 married males it was found that incidence of polygyny during ten years prior to 1961 was 5.06% among the Hindus, 4 31% among the Muslims. 4.44% among the Jain, 17.98 % among the tribals and 8.13% among the Buddhists.

ground. Even the creation of Pakistan had taken place through an agreement signed by our leaders who had the option to refuse putting their signatures on the same. The present day Muslims in India can not be held responsible for this.

It was however very clear that a common Hindu in our villages and towns, is not so much brothered about these pernicious questions, unless he has been indoctrinated by interested quarters. These questions are raised by either by chauvinists, representing a class having vested interest in communal conflicts, or by some well meaning, but misguided people without adequate knowledge of the character of Indian society and its segments.

Let us recall the socio-economic background of the area that could be ignited on Ramjanam Bhoomi-Babri Masjid issue. The density of population in Bhagalpur is 469 per sq. km. against 402 in Bihar and 207 in India. The percentage of urban population in the district is 11.72 against 12.47 in Bihar and 20.40 in India which indicates a very low level of its industrial development. About 95% of the trade and commerce in the district is in the hands of the people from outside the state. The population of this trading commnnity namely the Maswaris has increased three-fold through migration during the last two decades. The forward castes constituting about 10.00% of the population control over 90.00% of the agricultural land. Only two of the forward castes namely Bhumihar and Rajput constituting 7.00% of the total population of the state own 78.67% of the total agricultural land. All India figure, according to 1981 census, of the landless agricultural labour is 8.34%, it is 35.50% in Bihar and 41.42% in Bhagalpur. Though bonded labour has been legally abolished it continues in Bhagalpur. Bigger and more resourceful agriculturists defy minimum wages act. A large percentage of the people, particularly belonging to scheduled castes do not own land even to build their huts on and squat here and there. Many at the lower level of the society, particularly the landless, migrate seasonally to neighbouring states and to distant Punjab and Assam to escape the hardship and tyranny at home.

Growing consciousness among the backward castes constituting 69% of the total population of Bhagalpur as evidenced by their sweeping the last panchayat elections and a frustrating effect on the local educated unemployed youth raising slogans against the trading community from outside the state had an effect of creating alarm among the commercial class. This would go to show that a situation as this can be an easy prey to the designs of political parties who hold some promise of defusing the inter-caste tension through some methods including communalisation.

Communalisation of the society through creating a rift between Hindus and Muslims, for political purpose, has been among the objectives of certain organised and resourceful groups in the country and they have endeavoured to utilise the divergence of the two cultures for the furtherence of their objectives. The evidence of earliest endeavour in the direction is found in the works of British administrator historians who were largely motivated by the urge on their part to keep Indian Society as much divided as possible with the object of strengthening their hold on the country. These include Sir Henry Elliot[15] (1866), who devoted several volumes of his work to enumerate the conflicts between the 'foreign' medieval rulers against the Hindu 'natives'. F.W. Thomas[16] (1892) dwelt on the divergent nature of the cultural systems of Hindus and Musiims that lay at the root of imagined and supposed conflicts. M. Titus[17] (1930) observes that the causes of conflicts and tensions between Hindus and Muslims in recent history lie in their divergent beliefs and communal aspirations.

15. Vide K.A. Nizami, Politics and Society During Early Medieval Period ; Vol. 1, with reference to Henry Elliot and John Dawnson's 'History of India' Vol. 1, (Sir Henry Elliot's original preface pp. XIX-XXI), London 1962.

16. 'Mutual Influence of Mohammadans and Hindus in India ; , 1892.

17. 'Indian Islam : A Religious History of Islam in India ; London, 1930.

A host of other scholars, either British or under British influence such as J. Sarkar[18] (1924), P. Spear [19] (1958), A.L. Basham[20] (1958), R.C. Majumdar[21] (1960) developed an attitude that impelled them to over-emphasise the divergence over-looking the intimate socio-cultural relationthip between the two communities of very durable nature.[22] What was missed in these so called scholarly works was the well defined policy of 'divide et impera' of the powerful colonial rulers so unhesitatingly expressed and vigorously pursued by its administrative machinery involving the Duke of Willington, the Governor General the Viceroys with all the resources at their command. They made constant endeavours to induce conflict between Hindus and Muslims,[23] which was astonishingly non-existent to a British observer[24] until early nineteenth century.

Swamy Shradhanand's sudden change from his championship of the *Khilafat* movement to the leadership of the *Suddhi*

18. Sir Jadu Nath Sarkar, 'A History of Aurangzeb', Calcutta 1924.
19. Perceval Spear, 'India, Pakistan and the West', London 1958.
20. A.L. Basham, 'The Indian Sub-continent in Historical Prospective', London 1958.
21. R.C. Majumdar, 'The History and Culture of the Indian People', Bombay, 1960.
22. M.K.A. Siddiqui : 'Muslim Society and Culture in India : Their Regional Variability and Inter-community Relationship'. (Pub).
23. "I cannot close my eyes to the belief" wrote Lord Ellenborough in 1843, "that this race (Musalman) is fundamentally hostile to us and therefore our trne policy is to conciliate the Hindus" (N.G. Barrier : 1976 : 169-70).

    "Divide et impera" should be the motto of our Indian administration whether political, civil or military" wrote a British Scholar under name-de-plume 'Carnaticus' in Asiatic journal dated : May 1821, Ibid.

    "Lord Elphinstone, Governor of Bombay, in a minute dated May 14, 1858 finds himself in full agreement with the Dukc of Wellington over pursuing a policy of divide and rule. Ibid. p. 168.
24. Wabter Hamilton. 'East India Gazette' 1928, Aden & Co., London. (First published in 1813).

movement, aiming at the conversion of the Muslims to Hinduism, his writing of a blasphemous book "Rangila Rasool' to inflict grevious wounds to Muslim sentiments, his assassination by a Muslim fanatic, also Pandit Kalicharan's "Vichitr Jeevan" and Gian Chander's 'Worthman' to offend Muslim religious feelings, all appeared in twenties just after the Khilafat movement. These events followed by a series of communal riots in the states where first semi-responsible governments were formed under the Act of 1935. These were obviously engineered by the Colonial power through their agents to subvert the freedom movement. The hidden hands of the dominant power did their best to engineer a sense of fright of cultural subordination among the disillusioned Muslim minority and a section of the community was led to the path of separatism. The emergence of Pakistan gave a new dimension to communalism in the country. Communal feelings were raised to a new height. Despite widespread riots that had preceded and followed the division of the country, the dust of tension and conflict did not persist indefinitely or for a long time. It subsided gradually, though it did not vanish altogether.

It may be clear that the emergence of communalism has very largely been due to the needs of the vested interest to serve its purpose. The British needed communal tension to forestall the freedom movement to prolong their rule over the country. They did the ground work and laid it on a sound foundation, through a communal perception of history, through various economic measures to create disbalance and tension in the society, through their linguistic policy etc. It is evident that unlike the Mughals who had a vested interest in communal peace and harmony, the British had a vested interest in communal disharmony. Thus communalism became an important feature of a section of the society particularly the English educated urban middle class which was indoctrinated for generations. The communalism of this class was not always manifest but certainly latent. The village folk remained comparatively free from communalism.

In post-independence period communalism may be observed to be assuming a role, somewhat different from what it did in the pre-independence period, in the typical social situation in the country. The social stratification forming the ideological basis of the traditional Hindu society which has operated for centuries, has led to the concentration of wealth and power in the hands of the numerically smaller section of the society, identified as forward and trading castes.

A growing consciousness, among the numerically dominant backward and scheduled castes, of their continued economic deprivation and of their distance from political and administrative power coupled with the growing assertion to gain democratic egalitarianism makes the numerically small but privileged forward castes somewhat uneasy and unnerved. Only a few steps of the backward and scheduled castes in the direction of reducing the gap is viewed with alarm by the privileged forward. The possibility of bridging the gulf and attainment of equality does not fit in the world view of the privileged twice born and goes against their class interest. The tension between the two is inevitable but at the same time a perpetual conflict that may threaten to tear apart the caste society is also inconceivable by the reflective section of the society. There is an easy way of crying wolf and attempting at a solution that may have a harmonising effect on the caste society, in terms of the forward and to keep them saddled with power. Here is the 'functional' role for communalism in the negative sense. There are enough of historical materials to build tension against a minority with a distinct cultural boundary of their own.

The growing strength of the ultra rightist forces in the state and the emergence of anti Muslim Hindu militant organisations[25] as also the increasing number and ferocity of anti-Muslim riots have kept pace with the ever increasing assertion

25. Some of the organisations are : (1) R.S.S., (2) Vishwa Hindu Parishad, (3) Shiv Sena, (4) Bajrang Dal. (5) Shiv Shakti Dal, (6) Arya Vir Dal, (7) Punjab Hindu Sanghatan, (8) Vishal Hindu Samudaya, (9), Youth Volunteer Corps. Some of the older Hindu socic-political organisations include (10) Hindu Mahasabha, (11) Bharat Sevak Samaj, (12) Arya Samaj etc.

of the deprived Hindu castes to obtain their democratic rights including their demand for reservation of jobs. The violent agitation over the decision to implement Mondal Commission report on reservation throughout the country is only a recent history.

The anti-Muslim stance of uncompromising nature is quite obviously to inflame passions and to lead the people to a particular direction for the purpose of gaining political power for continued exploitation of the underdog. Inflaming passions against Muslims is an easy way to divert attention from issues that emanate from socio-economic backwardness by capitalising on deeply entrenched communal perception of history into the collective psyche of the people. As the anti-cow slaughter movement and anti-Urdu agitation of mid seventies aimed at building tension against Muslims did not have the desired effect the temple issue was carefully picked up for the purpose. The Rathyatra of the B.J.P. leader in October 1990, for example, on the occasion of the first anniversary of *Shilanias* or ceremonial laying of the foundation of Ramjanam Bhumi temple on the site of the Babri Masjid in Ayodhya, leaving in its trail an orgy of anti-Muslim violence in many scores of cities, was claimed to be an act of integration of the society, meaning thereby the Hindu society. The claimants in fact meant that the *yatra* was intended to forge unity in the Hindu fold that was seriously divided on the issue of the implementation of the Mondal Commission report on reservation.

Thus one of the tactical measures forging Hindu unity or at least for submerging inter-caste tension and conflict employed by them is to find out a common enemy. The Muslims are available to serve as scapegoats and Muslim endeavour for self preservation provides their antagonists with readily available pretext for violence. Communalism or anti-Muslim postures have come to assume a 'functional' role to play in a society inherently opposed to democratic egalitarianism in serving as an instrument of countering democratic process. It helps forestalling healthy political development and endeavours to defeat struggle for social justice. Caste in its changing role in the wake of political modernisation endeavours to assert itself and subverts democracy. It does not hesitate to adopt even utterly inhuman role. But will it achieve ultimate success ?

6

Epilogue

A definite change in the pattern of inter-caste relationship in recent years is quite obvious. Ever increasing frequency of caste conflicts, persecution of Harijans by upper and intermediate castes, emergence of caste senas, virulent movements for and against job reservations on the basis of caste and similar other activities involving caste, so frequently reported in the national press, provide clear indications of the direction of change in relationship between castes. The change had been occurring as a slow and systematic process both in attitudes and behaviour and of late it has accelerated its pace at a rate much faster than ever before. The change is from pacific acceptance of one's superior or inferior position or status in life as determined by the tradition, to a state of assertiveness, confrontation, conflict and violence. The behaviour reflects determined endeavour either to deny equality or to achieve it at any cost by respective interests. The attitudes have also changed characterising either a strong urge for preservation and strengthening the superior position or assertiveness to elevation and equalisation of the inferior socio-economic status depending upon the position the caste occupies in the hierarchy. Obviously the change is sought to be brought about not through the culturally prescribed method of *Karma* or through social mobility movement of Sanskritization, but through the non-traditional path taking its cue from democracy and modernisation.

Though the natural urge among the people suffering from birth determined inferiority, to achieve higher status, was not altogether absent and there are evidences to prove that they have in the past questioned the validity of the philosophy advocating the unalterability of their status during lifetime, quite a number of factors were responsible for development of passivity and unassertiveness. The acceptance of birth assigned status was the result of a deeply ingrained religious feeling and a discipline the people were subjected to for a very long period.

The origin of this development that has led to the polarisation of forces seeking a redefinition of inter-relationship on the one hand and opposition to change the status quo on the other, can be traced to the introduction of democracy in our political system. Introduction of the system encouraging a slow process of participatory democracy demanded sharing of political power and national resources on more equitable basis, while the system of caste based on institutionalised inequality provided a mental framework that resisted attempts to undo inequality. The operation of the system of caste, as it had shaped the society, had made the upper strata of the society coinciding roughly with the upper castes, formidably powerful in terms of the control of resources and political power which it was not ready to share on equitable basis. This strata was not prepared to loosen its control over the total society and was opposed to its socio-economic emancipation, uplift and ultimate equalisation. This opposition was not explicit nor was it loudly spelt out and the enlightened leadership of the upper caste continued to verbalise its commitment to ameleorate the condition of the deprived castes, but whatever action it took in the direction was inadequate. The gulf between the two got infact widened instead of getting bridged. In firmly holding their privileges the upper castes were not only protecting their socio-economic interests but were also upholding their religio-cultural belief in the doctrine of *Karma* that had shaped their mind. It is also interesting that instead of launching a movement for undoing or modifying the system of caste, that lay at the root of their social degradation and economic plight, the underprivileded castes took the help of the very same institution to organise themselves to gain political power and economic justice. In doing so they were also not explicit, at least within the framework of modern democratic institutions like political parties. They were fighting for their democratic rights with weapons picked up from the armoury of caste.

This and many other factors would go to show that democratic institutions are merely formal and superficial while the traditional institution of the caste is more basic, real and fundamental. The frequency and intensity of caste conflicts also go to show that a non-violent social change through democratic process may be difficult because it militates against the deeply ingrained belief in inequality as inculcated by the doctrine of *Karma*. There is no significant movement against the basic philosophy underlying the system of caste, though quite a few, reformers have worked hard to remove some of the oppressive and inhuman features of the system largely of peripheral nature.

While democracy is based on the principle of equality caste does not accept equnality. It accepts people either high or low. It believes in dealing with people either as superior or inferior. Behaviourally the superiors are to be submitted to and the inferiors are to be subjected to subordination.

This does not mean to say that caste as an institution has been devoid of any merit and is to becondemned outright and that its rolei n elevating human society from a state of savagory is to be undermined. Caste has definitely played important role in carrying human civilization forward. It has however been observed to stop men half way on the road to progress (Hutton : 1946-69 : 123 with reference to P.N. Bose). Its ethos are opposed to modern participatory democracy, embracing all segments of society either in villages or in a larger combination, though castes manage their respective internal affairs democratically.

The formidability of the caste can be estimated from the fact that it is stronger than religious beliefs. The social habits of caste are inextricably tied up with religion (Hutton : 1946-69 : 125) and this gives caste added strength, as well as a motivation for self-preservation. Its formidability becomes all the more conspicuous when the upper castes have concentrated wealth and power and have reached a stage of development in which they are in full control of the situation. This state of development motivates the dominant to subvert a porticipatory democracy tending to bring about social justice and egalitarianism. Like most other institutions caste has a core, relatively unalterable, and a perephery which may accept change or modifications. In the wake of an onslaught the core is likely to assert. In the caste society there are segments which have vested interest in its preservation and are likely to react strongly in the interest of preservation of their prerogatives, while some others may direct their endeavour to bring an end to their exploitation. This explains the caste conflict that has conspicuously developed in recent years.

In a desperate bid for self-preservation and continued self-assertion, the vested interest in the caste society, constituting the privileged castes, is led to adopt methods to stem any move that is directed towards dislodging it from a position of dominance. Inter-caste conflict in the wake of the upsurge of lower castes provides a situation of this sort. In dealing with this situation the powerful interests in the system are led to adopt all means without considering the question of propriety, legitimacy or morality of such action. It has its own standard of morality based on the need to protect, defend and preserve its birth determined status which is believed to be divinely ordained. The internal violence or inter-caste conflict is projected outside the caste society and is carried beyond its boundaries. This necessity on the part of the caste, or the group, having wested interests in the system, largely explains a systematic communalisation of the society picking up Muslims, a significant minority as its target. Here is a community which is not prepared to accept an inferior position while the caste idioms assign it only a position which is subjected to subordination.

The violence is sought to be transferred beyond the boundary of the caste society to the Muslim minority for the purpose of diversion of the attention of the underprivileged and deprived castes by commonalising the atmosphere in order to side-track the urge or demand for social justice, the main cause of the inter-caste tension and conflict. This is also aimed at keeping the privileged saddled in power. The endeavours of the privileged in communalising the atmosphere only side-tracks the real issues of social justice and only postpones the inevitable. This side tracking of the problem of social justice will amount only to a postponement of the real issues only temporarily. The democratic institutions which have been introduced will continue to inspire the people to continue struggling for social justice. It may pave the way for another kind of combination between the Muslim minority and the numerically more dominant backward castes, based not on mere emotionality but on rationality and self-interest.

Bibliography

Aggarwal, Pratap, (1971) Caste Religion and Power, Shri Ram Centre for Industrial Relations.

Anant, Santokh Singh, (1978) "Changing caste—Hindu Attitudes Towards Harijans ; A Follow-up after four years in Cohesion and Conflict in Indian Society"—Main Currents in Indian Sociology, Vol. III; Ed. Giri Raj Gupta, Vikas Pub. House, New Delhi.

Atal, Yogesh, (1968) The Changing Frontiers of Caste, National Publishing House, New Delhi.

Barrier, N.G. (ed.), (1976) Roots of Communal Politics (Report of the Cownpur Riot Enquiry Committee, 1933) Delhi.

Basham, A.L., (1958) The Indian Sub-Continent in Historical Perspective London.

Bookman, L.M., (1978) "Hindus and Muslims : Communal Relations and Cultural Integration in Cohesion and Conflict in Indian Society"—Main Currents in Indian Society. 3rd Ed. Giri Raj Gupta; Vikas Pub. House, New Delhi.

Brass, Paul R., (1974) Language, Religion and Politics in North India, Cambridge University Press, London.

Brass, Paul R., (1984) Caste, Faction and Party in Indian Politics, Vol. 1; Faction and Party, Chanakya Publications, Delhi.

Buch, M.N., 1988 Review of Rajni Kothari's State Against Democracy in The Telegraph, dated : July 16.

Byrne, J. (1911) Bhagalpur District Gazette

Census of India 1931, Vol. III, Part II.

Census of India 1931, Vol. III, Bihar and Orissa.

Census of India 1981, Series 1, India, Paper 3 of 1984.

Census of India 1981, Series 4, Part IX.

Census of India 1981, Series 4, Part IV A.

Census of India 1981, Series 1, India, Paper 4, of 1984.

Census of India 1981, District Census Handbook, Bhagalpur, Parts XIII-A and B, Village and Town Directory.

Das, Arvind N., (1985) Bihar Society in Perspective, Roots of Regional Imbalance. Times of India, 25th October, 1985. Also 25th October, 1985.

Das, Suranjan, (1991) Communal Riots in Bengal 1905-1947 Oxford University Press, Calcutta.

Desai, I.P. and Others, (1985) Caste, Caste Conflict and Reservations, Ajanta Publications.

Elliot, Henry and Dawson, John, (1866) History of India Vol, I (Sir Henry Ellitot's original preface pp. XIX-XXI) London.

Hamilton, Webter, (1828) East India Gazette, Allen and Company, London.

Gupta, Giri Raj (ed.), (1978) Cohesion and Conflict in Modern India in Main Currents in Indias Sociology, Vol. III; Vikas Pub. House, New Delhi.

Jain, S.P., 1975 The Social Structure of Hindu-Muslim Community. National Publishers, Delhi.

Kothari, Rajni and Rashikesh Maru, (1965) "Caste and Secularism in India : Case Study of Caste Federation". Jr. of Asian Studies, 25 (November) 30-50.

Kothari, Rajni (ed). (1970) Caste in Indian Politics, Orient Longman, Delhi.

Kothari, Rajni, (1970) "Introduction" In Rajni Kothari (ed), Caste in Indian Politics, pp. 3-25; New Delhi; Orient Longman.

Mehta, Sushila, (1971) Social Conflicts in a Village Community. S. Chand and Co. Delhi.

Mishra, Upendra, (1986) Caste and Politics in India (A Study of Political Turmoil in Bihar), Uppal Publishing House; New Delhi.

Mukherjee, B.N., (1990) Tension and Tolerance in Pre-Islamic India. The Telegraph, Dated : 30.11.90 Calcutta.

Risley, H.H. (1891) Tribes and Castes of Bengal, Vo. I, Calcutta (Reprinted in 1981),

Rudolph, Llyod L, (1965) The Modernity of Tradition : The Democratic Incarnation of Caste in India. American Political Science Review, 59(4); 975-89.

Sarkar, Jadu Nath, (1924) A History of Aurangzeb, Calcutta.

Shakir, Moin, (1982) "Understanding the Framework of Caste Violence" in Contemporary India ; Socio-Economic and Political Process. Ed. Inamdar, N.R. and others. Continental Prakashan, Poona.

Schermerhorn, R.A., (1978) Social Mobility of three Minorities in India ; A quantitative Approach. (in Cohesion and Conflict in Modern India in Main Currents in Indian Sociology Vol. III) Ed. Giri Raj Gupta, Vikas Publishing House, New Delhi.

Silverberg, James, (1978) Social Categories Vs Organisations : Class Conflict in a Caste Structured System in Giri Raj Gupta (ed) Cohesion ond Conflict in Indian Society— Main Currents in Indian Sociology III: Vikas, New Delhi.

'Singh, N.K.,, (1772) Many Aspects of Caste Politics in India, Economic and Political Weekly, April, 8, 1972 pp. 748.

Singh. Yogendra, (1973) Modernisation of Indian Tradition, A Systematic Study of Social Change. Thomson Press.

Sinha, Sachidanand, (1973) The Internal Colony : A Case Study in Regional Exploitation; Sandhu Prakashan.

Schermenhorn, R.A., Communal Violence in India : A Case Study. Kalamanoo Michigan Consultative Committee of Indian Muslims, 76, III – 56 p,

Spear, Percival, 1953 India Pakistan and the West, London.

Sukla, Kiran, (1987) Caste Politics in India, Mittal Pub. Techno-Economic Survey of Bihar, Vol. I, National Council of Applied Economic Research, New Delhi, (Bombay : Asia Publishing House 1959).

Thapar, Romila, Mukhia Harbans and Chandra, Bipin, (1969) Communalism and the Writings of Indian History. Peoples' Publishing House. (Review by Shahid Amin in Seminar Jan. 1972).

Thomas, F.W., (1892) Mutual Influence of Mohammadans and Hindus in India, Cambridge.

Titus, Murray T., (1930) Indian Islam : A Religious History of Islam in India-London.

Index